# The Orthodox Jewish Wedding Planner

## Second Edition

Dr. Ephraim Horowitz

© 2011, Ephraim Horowitz, Ph.D.

Second Edition (2.15)

All rights reserved. No portion of this publication may be reproduced in any form without written permission from the author, except as mentioned below on page 13.

Cover illustrations by Mrs. Natanya Nudelman

Send comments to jewishweddings@mindspring.com.

ISBN 978-0-557-76450-1

*– To my wife, Bonnie…*

*I could not have planned it better.*

# Contents

## *PART I – Wedding Planning Concepts* .................................................................. *15*
### *I.1  High-Level Planning* ................................................................................. *17*
- I.1.1 Choosing a Date .................................................................................. 17
- I.1.2 Mesader Kiddushin .............................................................................. 19
- I.1.3 Wedding Costs ..................................................................................... 19
- I.1.4 Customs ................................................................................................ 23
- I.1.5 Documentation .................................................................................... 29

### *I.2  Selecting Vendors* ..................................................................................... *32*
- I.2.1 Selecting a Hall .................................................................................... 34
- I.2.2 Selecting a Caterer .............................................................................. 40
- I.2.3 Selecting a Florist ............................................................................... 47
- I.2.4 Selecting an Orchestra ....................................................................... 49
- I.2.5 Selecting a Photographer .................................................................. 51

### *I.3  Guests* ......................................................................................................... *54*
- I.3.1 Tracking Guests ................................................................................... 54
- I.3.2 Invitations ............................................................................................. 57
- I.3.3 Accommodations ................................................................................. 61
- I.3.4 Honorees ............................................................................................... 62

### *I.4  Help* ............................................................................................................. *65*

### *I.5  Detailed Planning* ..................................................................................... *67*
- I.5.1 Dressing Up .......................................................................................... 67
- I.5.2 Wedding Activities ............................................................................. 70
- I.5.3 Other Events ........................................................................................ 75
- I.5.4 What to Bring ...................................................................................... 78
- I.5.5 Wedding Day Schedule ...................................................................... 83
- I.5.6 After the Wedding .............................................................................. 86

## *PART II – Checklists* ............................................................................................. *87*
### *II.1  Timing Checklist* ...................................................................................... *88*
### *II.2  Choosing a Date Checklist* .................................................................... *90*
### *II.3  Wedding Cost Checklists* ....................................................................... *91*
### *II.4  Customs Checklist* ................................................................................... *92*
### *II.5  Selecting a Hall Checklist* ..................................................................... *94*

| | | |
|---|---|---|
| *II.6* | *Selecting a Caterer Checklist* | *97* |
| *II.7* | *Selecting a Florist Checklist* | *99* |
| *II.8* | *Selecting an Orchestra Checklist* | *101* |
| *II.9* | *Selecting a Photographer Checklists* | *103* |
| *II.10* | *Guest List Sample* | *107* |
| *II.11* | *Seating List Sample* | *109* |
| *II.12* | *Invitations and Benchers Checklists* | *111* |
| *II.13* | *Wardrobe Checklist* | *114* |
| *II.14* | *Paperwork Checklist* | *115* |
| *II.15* | *Accommodations Checklists* | *116* |
| *II.16* | *Participants Checklist* | *119* |
| *II.17* | *Announcer Responsibilities Checklist* | *122* |
| *II.18* | *What to Bring Checklist* | *123* |
| *II.19* | *Sheva Brachos Checklists* | *124* |
| *Part III – Blessings* | | *127* |
| *III.1* | *Badeken* | *129* |
| *III.2* | *Chuppah* | *130* |
| *III.3* | *Sheva Brachos* | *132* |
| *III.4* | *Benching for the Sheva Brachos Meal* | *133* |
| *Part IV – Reference* | | *135* |
| *IV.1* | *Glossary* | *137* |
| *IV.2* | *Artwork Credits* | *140* |
| *IV.3* | *Citations* | *140* |

## Checklists

For quick reference, all checklists are listed on page 141.

## Blessings

Blessings 1 – Fathers to the Kallah at the Badeken ........................................... 129
Blessings 2 – Fathers to the Kallah at the Badeken – The Priestly Blessing.... 129
Blessings 3 – When the Chosson Arrives at the Chuppah................................. 130
Blessings 4 – When the Chosson Arrives at the Chuppah (German Custom).. 130
Blessings 5 – When the Kallah Arrives at the Chuppah.................................... 130
Blessings 6 – Erusin........................................................................................... 130
Blessings 7 – The Chosson Gives the Kallah the Ring ..................................... 131
Blessings 8 – Before Breaking the Glass........................................................... 131
Blessings 9 – German Custom before Breaking Glass...................................... 131
Blessings 10 – Sheva Brachos ............................................................................. 132
Blessings 11 – Introduction to Sheva Brachos Benching .................................... 133

## Figures

Figure 1 – Meal Arrangement Options ............................................................... 44
Figure 2 - Sample Logo ....................................................................................... 59
Figure 3 – International Response Coupon......................................................... 61
Figure 4 – Chuppa Ceremony Positions ............................................................. 72
Figure 5 – Wedding Day Schedule ..................................................................... 85

## Photos

Photo 1 – Kallah's Chair ................................................................................... 21
Photo 2 – Bais Faiga - Lakewood, New Jersey ................................................ 34
Photo 3 – Badeken - Escorting the Chosson to the Kallah............................... 36
Photo 4 – Center Aisle Leading to Chuppah .................................................... 36
Photo 5 – New Couple's Grand Entrance ......................................................... 37
Photo 6 – Watermelon Swans........................................................................... 40
Photo 7 – Flowers ............................................................................................. 47
Photo 8 – Trumpet ............................................................................................ 49
Photo 9 – Photographer .................................................................................... 51
Photo 10 – Seating Cards ................................................................................... 56
Photo 11 – Tripping-Hazard Train...................................................................... 73
Photo 12 – Through the Arches .......................................................................... 74
Photo 13 – Sheva Brachos .................................................................................. 76
Photo 14 – Nifty Plate Smashers ........................................................................ 79
Photo 15 – Shtick ................................................................................................ 82

## Acknowledgements

This guide contains ideas and suggestions collected over several years of organizing and attending weddings. Many hints and tips contained herein come to you by the good graces of friends and relatives with whom I have shared many simchas. I regret that I cannot name them all individually (though some may be happier that I didn't).

This is my first book intended for public dissemination. One thing I have learned is how many mistakes can fit into a very small space. I am greatly indebted to my dear friend Jay Cherniak and my loving mother, Iris Chester, for weeding out many of them. Each has over thirty years of professional editorial experience that they applied generously to this project, contributing much to its final state.

Much appreciation is due to my daughter, Natanya Nudelman, for the beautiful artwork on the cover. You may not be able to *tell* a book by its cover but you can *sell* a book by its cover!

I would also like to thank my daughter-in-law, Naomi Horowitz, an experienced wedding coordinator, for reviewing the material included herein and providing several important tips.

In compiling information about various customs for the second edition, I had the great pleasure of consulting with many rebeeim. In particular, I would like to thank (in alphabetical order) Rabbi Eli Backman, Rabbi Zechariah Gelley, Rabbi Menachem Goldberger, Rabbi Emanuel Goldfciz, Rabbi Naftoli Hexter, Rabbi Yaakov Horowitz, Mr. Menachem Lasdun and Rabbi Yisroel (Sidney) Strauss. To all of you, I extend my profound appreciation for your knowledge, attentiveness and encouragement.

# Introduction

Organization – To some it is the cold, cruel codification of place and time into a still and lifeless arrangement. To others it is the comfort and calm of knowing that everything is in its place and all is well. Once, when I was about five years old, I asked my father for a piece of paper. I guess I just wanted something on which to color. He gave me the first thing he found nearby, which, since he was an engineer, turned out to be a piece of graph paper. I was stunned by its symmetry and order. I instantly wanted to write things in the boxes and check them off and draw lines to make interesting graphs. It seemed so perfect. Ever since, I have been striving to put my life into little boxes. My wife (also very organized) and I have lists for everything. Every Shabbos we prepare our home according to our Shabbos list. We have several travel lists depending on the type of trip we are taking. I don't walk out the door in the morning without consulting my "out-the-door-list". Nuts and bolts are in little drawers. Medications are sorted by function and type. Keys are tagged and hung in a row. All receipts, bills and documents are filed appropriately. All this may give you comfort knowing that you are dealing with an expert or, conversely, it may be an incentive to avoid this insanity while you still can.

Planning a wedding is a daunting task. There is so much to do. The myriads of details and complicated timing can seem overwhelming. This guide is intended to lay out those details in an orderly fashion and to facilitate the process from beginning to end.

The emphasis here is on planning, so hints are given to make things run smoother and to save money. I do not delve deeply into the complexity, significance and beauty of our customs and religious laws. Others have done a great job in this area, such as Rabbi Aryeh Kaplan with *Made in Heaven,* which contains a wealth of insights into the laws and customs of a Jewish wedding as well as many practical ideas; and Rabbi Maurice Lamm with *The Jewish Way in Love and Marriage,* which is a treasure of information on the Jewish approach to marriage. Both are very readable.

Note that my focus is on *Orthodox* Jewish weddings; therefore many assumptions are made regarding the wedding plans. Also, I reference many Hebrew and Yiddish terms related to Jewish weddings. They are defined in a glossary toward the end of this guide on page 137.

To be as comprehensive as possible, I tried to include almost everything that one might do to arrange a wedding. This is not to say that you must, or even should, do *all* of them. Several things listed here are optional, as should be clear from the context. Hopefully, I have covered almost all of the preparations you will need to achieve the best possible wedding.

This guide has two main parts. The first describes, in detail, the wedding planning process, including hints and tips where applicable. The second contains planning checklists that succinctly list all of the steps mentioned in the first part. Each part complements the other. Read the first part to get the whole story and then use the checklists to track each step of the way. These two parts are followed by a collection of blessings and songs related to the wedding ceremony. Finally, the guide concludes with various references, including a glossary of terms used herein.

Organization is wonderful, but you may be planning a wedding with the cooperation of others who may not share your orderly enthusiasm. Take it in stride. Clearly designate responsibilities and then focus on your part. So, if the others don't book the hall, and the caterer is not squared away, so the wedding ends up in your driveway, and the guests are eating cold pizza, feel comfortable knowing that you have decorated it precisely as planned with beautiful flowers, and the couple should, nonetheless, live happily ever after.

Though this guide tries to cover every known aspect of a Jewish wedding, one can never be fully prepared. The power may fail and the roof may cave in. King David writes in Psalms 33:10, "Many are the thoughts in the heart of Man, but it is the counsel of Hashem that will stand." One can never forestall every eventuality, and we will never know what G-d has in store for us. But if we plan carefully with the intent to fulfill the Will of our Creator, may He assist us in our endeavors.

Remember that planning a wedding is a means to an end, i.e., the wedding. Remember also that the wedding is a means to an end, i.e., the marriage. Your most important checklist should have only one check-box.

**Checklist 1 – The Main Point**

| Done | Item |
|------|------|
|      | All preparations should lead to an atmosphere of love and understanding that will start the new couple on a path to a beautiful, marriage building a trustworthy house among the nation of Israel for the sake of Hashem. |

## *Legend*

This guide contains special topics of interest. Various icons are used to highlight them.

**Money-Saving Tip** – There are several ways to save money with proper wedding planning. This icon will alert you to those opportunities. Many of them relate to borrowing or renting certain wedding necessities from gemachs or other organizations.

**Bright Idea** – This icon highlights things that are significant but easily overlooked as well as clever little suggestions that may help you.

**Caution** – This indicates problems that you should try to avoid. I have seen many of the mishaps mentioned herein. A little planning may help you avoid some of them.

**Personal Opinion** – This points out my personal opinion about a topic (some may call them pet peeves). Although this entire guide is my personal opinion, these opinions are all the more so. Feel free to disagree. You'll be in good company!

**Decision Point** – This indicates a point at which you will need to make a significant decision as to how you want your wedding to run. In truth, most of this guide is about choices. But these are some you might not have considered.

## *Copyright*

Like any other printed work, this guide represents a significant amount of time, effort and financial investment and is copyrighted. All rights are reserved and no reproduction in any form may be made for any purpose. However, there is one exception. Copies of the checklists may be made for the *specific* wedding for which this guide was purchased. So if, for example, you intend to interview six photographers rather than four, or you would like to give an extra copy of your honoree list to your wedding coordinator, then permission is hereby granted for that purpose.

# PART I – Wedding Planning Concepts

*Part I – Wedding Planning Concepts*

# I.1 High-Level Planning

This section describes many of the initial decisions that must be made early on. These decisions often involve more cooperation between the families. Coordination up front will allow each family to work on their portion with more autonomy and efficiency.

## I.1.1 Choosing a Date✓

Mazel Tov! They're engaged! Whether you are thinking "It's about time!" or "Already?" we need to get going on making this wedding happen.

If the first question was "Will you marry me?" then the second question had better be "When?" It is important from a relationship perspective that the wedding commitment be real and definite in terms of a time frame. It is also crucial from a planning perspective since all other activities will revolve around the wedding date. Selecting a date and time is challenging. Several considerations are involved.

### *General Time Frame*

Before setting a specific date, determine a target time frame. In Biblical and Talmudic times, a couple would be partially married right away (erusin) and then the woman would be given up to twelve months to prepare necessities for the final wedding stage (nesuin). Nowadays, the halachic stages of erusin and nesuin both transpire under the chuppah, one right after the other. Present day engagements, which are not as legally binding, typically range from a few months to over a year. When choosing a general time period for the wedding, consider the following:

- Is there enough time to prepare? The minimum reasonable time to prepare a wedding is about three months, though I have seen it done in less time.
- Will school, seminary, or other previously scheduled weddings make it difficult for guests? You will not be able to accommodate everyone's schedule, but you might want to consider the more significant guests such as close family, certain rabbis and special friends.
- Will weather be an issue? If you live in a very cold climate or an area with seasonally severe weather, think about how that may interfere with the wedding.

### *Specific Days*

The specific day of the wedding is very important. Here are some things to keep in mind.

- Choosing a date close to a holiday may make it difficult to prepare and difficult for family members to travel. On the other hand, if guests are coming from afar for the holidays anyway, then it might be easier for them to stay a while longer for a wedding rather than come back at another time.
- Jewish law and customs preclude weddings from occurring on certain days. Some of them are:

---

✓ See Checklist 3 – Choosing a Date, page 82.

- Shabbos
- Jewish holidays (except for Chanukah)
- Fast days
- The three weeks between the 17th of Tamuz and the 9th of Av
- The period between Passover and Shevuoth (varying customs)

In general, check with your rabbi to ensure that the date you have chosen conforms to Jewish law.

## *Day of the Week*

Certain days of the week may be better than others for a wedding. In prewar Europe, weddings would start on Friday afternoon so as to combine the wedding meal with the Shabbos meal. This was done to save money, since people were very poor. Today, people get married almost any day of the week with the exception of Friday and Shabbos. There are varying customs that consider certain days of the week or portions of the month more auspicious than others.

Sunday is a popular day for several reasons. Clearly, it is a time when many people are off work and school. Note, however, that many items such as the hall, caterer and band may cost more on Sundays. Federal holidays have the same trade-offs. They have the advantage of giving guests who live far away extra travel time but the disadvantages of crowded travel conditions and higher travel costs.

 A weekday wedding and/or out-of-season wedding could save you money. Note, however, that in larger communities, there may not be an out-of-season period.

## *Time of Day*

The specific time of the wedding will, to some extent, depend on the specific day. Since the chosson and kallah fast on the wedding day, an earlier wedding is easier for them. However, the wedding can't be too early since there is so much to prepare on that day. Expect to arrive at the hall up to five hours in advance. Thus a wedding cannot start much before 1:00 p.m.

 An earlier wedding will make it easier for guests to catch return flights to faraway places.

If you are planning a weekday wedding, it should start in the evening to allow local guests to arrive after work and school. Here again, it should start as early as possible. Guests tend to leave in large numbers as the hour gets late. A reasonable starting time would be 5 p.m. A starting time of 7 p.m. is already late.

As with the day itself, some Jewish customs give preference to certain times within the day.

*Part I – Wedding Planning Concepts*

## I.1.2 Mesader Kiddushin

The officiating rabbi at the wedding is the mesader kiddushin. Throughout this guide, unqualified references to a rabbi refer to the mesader kiddushin. It is crucial to choose a rabbi early on who can answer the many questions that will arise. As a rule, the mesader kiddushin comes from the chosson's side. He may be the chosson's rabbi from yeshiva, the head of the chosson's yeshiva, or the rabbi from the chosson's family's shul.

This decision must be made early. The mesader kiddushin may have input or preferences on many aspects of the wedding.

There are several very important religious matters that have to be factored into the planning of a wedding. For instance, the chosson and kallah will need to be instructed in religious family matters, including ritual immersion for the kallah, which may impact the wedding date. The rabbi should be consulted on this as well.

Selecting the mesader kiddushin is included in Checklist 4 with other issues related to the scope of the wedding. This is appropriate since the mesader kiddushin will set the religious tone for the wedding.

Note: If the mesader kiddushin must travel to get to the wedding, it is expected that his travel fees will be reimbursed by the families making the wedding. See the next section.

## I.1.3 Wedding Costs✓

The Talmud states that there is no wedding without controversy. Most often controversy revolves around money. However, differences can be minimized by agreeing on the scope of the wedding and clearly delineating financial responsibilities.

⚖ Though this guide contains lots of innovative ways to spend money, many of them are optional. Consider the long-term benefit of helping the new couple start out on a firm financial footing against the brief enjoyment of a lavish wedding. Sometimes these decisions can be tough and unpopular. Good luck!

### *The Basics*

A major consideration is the general location of the wedding. Most often, the wedding is held near the city of the parents of the kallah, though this is not always the case. The choice of location will impact most of the other decisions.

The size of the wedding, i.e., the number of guests, is another major factor in determining the total cost. Initially the parties should agree on a rough estimate for the total number of guests (to within the nearest 50).

It is a good idea to discuss the overall wedding atmosphere. Some people prefer weddings that are very nicely appointed, while others prefer weddings that are decidedly simple. One

---

✓ See Checklist 4 – Wedding Scope and Checklist 5 – Wedding Cost Details, page 83.

family or the other may not have a preference either way, but it is better to find out earlier rather than later. If you are planning a wedding in some far off, exotic place (colloquially known as a *destination wedding*), the complexity will increase, and the number of guests will decrease. The total cost may be more or less than for a wedding closer to home. Orthodox Jewish couples do not typically plan destination weddings, and this guide does not include the additional complications of planning them.

## *Divide and Conquer*

For older couples, more of the expenses may be borne by the couple themselves. For younger couples, the parents, if willing and able, pick up most of the expenses. In any case, decisions about dividing the cost need to be made early on.

Deciding who pays for what may be difficult, but once agreed upon, it clears the way for simpler planning. There are no rules for who pays for what but there is a common scheme dubbed FLOP, an acronym for those items paid for by the chosson's family.

- F = Flowers
- L = Liquor
- O = Orchestra
- P = Photography

The other major expenses, i.e., the hall and the catering, would then be paid for by the kallah's family. Note that this still leaves some additional unassigned expenses, such as:

- Invitations (printing and mailing)
- Benchers

If the mesader kiddushin must travel to get to the wedding, then his arrangements should be provided for him. If he represents the chosson's side, as is typical, then the chosson's family should provide for his travel expenses.

None of this is written in stone and points can be negotiated amicably if all involved proceed in good faith.

Note that the FLOP system is not always equitable. For instance, if the chosson's side has a very large number of guests, then it would not be reasonable for the kallah's side to pay for all of them. One possible resolution is for the kallah's family to pay for a certain number of guests, with the chosson's side paying for any extras from their side.

☺ Once the delineations have been made, each side should be given purview over its own responsibilities. Each party should be sensitive to the privacy and dignity of the other in regard to how little or how much is paid for each item. I am particularly *not* fond of the argument that a large expense on one item by one party necessitates a comparable expense by the other party on some other item.

*Part I – Wedding Planning Concepts*

($) Note that many items can be borrowed from gemachs. A gemach is a service which provides items for free or for a minimal charge. If your community does not have gemachs, it may pay to travel to another, nearby community that does. Throughout the rest of this guide, I will mention gemachs for common wedding items. However, newer ones with more unusual things are opening continually, so stay alert.

## *Important Details*

Depending on your community and the hall and caterer you use, certain items may come from various places. Any of the following may come from the hall, the caterer, the florist or some other organization such as a shul. They may be part of an overall cost or may need to be acquired separately. Specifically, determine who is providing…

- The chuppah
- The mechitza
- The chosson's and kallah's chairs

(💡) Be sure to find out exactly what the chuppah and mechitza will look like and how much they will cost. The chuppah may be as simple as four wooden poles with a tallis on top held up by volunteers; or it may be an elaborate fixture set permanently in place. Similarly, the mechitza may range from something as simple as sheets on poles, to slatted wood dividers to arrangements of potted trees. Make sure that what is offered meets your religious, esthetic and financial needs. The chuppah should be large enough for the mothers to escort the kallah as she circles the chosson. The platform upon which the chuppah stands or the area around it should be larger to accommodate all the participants, as discussed in section I.5.2., p. 70.

Special chairs will be mentioned several times throughout this guide. The kallah customarily sits on a large, ornate chair at the badeken to emphasize the fact that she is a queen for the day. Those that I have seen are typically white wicker and may be decorated with flowers or covered with satin. Sometimes the chosson and kallah sit on similar chairs during the meal. Like the chuppah, they may be provided by the hall, caterer, florist or someone else. Unlike the chuppah, they are not an absolute necessity. Regular chairs may be used.

**Photo 1 – Kallah's Chair**

You will need to determine who will provide other items as well. These may not be expensive but nonetheless will have to be considered.

- Candles for the parents during the procession (if you will be using them)
- The glass and wine used under the chuppah

- 21 -

*The Orthodox Jewish Wedding Planner*

## *Overtime*

Weddings take months to plan and a few fleeting hours to pass. At the last moment you may be inclined to extend the celebration. Think about this far in advance. First, consider the cost of extending the services you have hired. The hall, caterer, photographer and orchestra will want compensation for overtime, and that compensation will not be cheap. Additional costs will accrue for all parties. Second, consider the guests who may want to participate in the sheva brachos at the end of the meal but may not be able to stay if the affair drags on. Decide up front if the celebration will extend beyond the scheduled time and who will be responsible for the extra cost.

## *Gifts*

There are numerous customs regarding gifts that the chosson traditionally gives to the kallah, and the kallah to the chosson, the chosson's family to the kallah, the kallah's family to the chosson, etc.

Strict customs about gift giving can be a burden to new family relationships. It is better if no one expects gifts, and everyone appreciates what they get. As King Solomon says, "He who hates gifts shall live" (Proverbs 15:27). I have listed a few here that I have heard of, but I did not include a checklist. The list seems to grow every time you look. Note that cash is often better since the young couple can then get what they really want and need.

### Chosson (or his family) to Kallah
- Engagement bracelet (if engagement ring is not ready)
- Engagement ring
- Wedding ring
  - The only REAL obligatory gift
  - Must belong to the chosson
- Pearl necklace
- Candlesticks
- Sheitel
- Siddur
- Flowers for the Shabbos Kallah and Vort. See section I.5.3, p. 75.

### Kallah (or her family) to Chosson
- Tallis (very common)
- Kittel
- Jewish books, often a set of the Talmud
- Dress wristwatch
- Wedding ring (atypical at a Jewish wedding)
- Kiddush cup

### Families to Others
- Financial gift to the shadchun, if one was involved; otherwise a gift to those who orchestrated the meeting of the couple.

- Financial gift to the mesader kiddushin

Additionally, anyone who helps in the planning and execution of the wedding should be thanked appropriately.

# I.1.4 Customs✓

The various customs surrounding a Jewish wedding are innumerable. This section includes as many as I could find, but there are surely more. The list here ranges from differences in halacha to regional customs and simple preferences. The purpose of describing them here and listing them later is to give you the tools to discuss them beforehand with all those involved and thereby alleviate unforeseen conflicts near or at the wedding.

Note that customs vary widely in importance. Consult your mesader kiddushin as to which customs must be fulfilled in a certain way. For those customs which allow for discretion, choose the path of most peace and harmony. Note also that some customs that originated with one group have become widely accepted among others.

## *Major Custom Communities*

Though difficult to classify precisely, here we divide the Jewish community into four major communities – Ashkenazim, Sephardim, Chassidim and German.

**Ashkenazim** are Jews who hail from Eastern Europe. About 70% of Jews worldwide are Ashkenazim. The more proper term would be Litvaks, which is Yiddish for Lithuanians, but in this guide I use the more colloquial, though less precise term for ease of understanding.

**Sephardim** are Jews from Southern Europe, Northern Africa, the Middle East and the Orient. The word Sepharad is the Hebrew word for Spain.

**Chassidim** also come from Eastern Europe but follow specific customs of Chassidic dynasties, all of which trace their spiritual origins back to founder of Chassidus, the Baal Shem Tov, who lived in the 1700s. Though the other major groups have a range of customs, Chassidic groups are probably the most diverse. Being that Lubavitch (Chabad) is one of the largest Chassidic groups, mention is made where their customs differ from those of other Chassidim.

**German** Jews, as the name implies, come from Germany. In truth, the word Ashkenaz was the Hebrew word for Germany for at least 1000 years. German Jews themselves refer to their specific customs as Ashkenaz. But in this guide, to avoid confusion with the colloquial use of Ashkenaz as referring to Eastern European Jews, we will use the term Germanic to refer to German customs.

As with the other groups, there are differences among various German communities. Of significant note are the efforts of Machon Moreshet Ashkenaz – an organization which is

---

✓ See Checklist 6 – Customs, page 84.

working to reinstate many older German customs which have fallen into disuse since World War II. See Web site [4], p. 140. However, since the vast majority of German Jews do not follow these older customs, I have omitted them from this guide.

**Jerusalem,** as the heart of the Jewish world, also has special customs for weddings. However, weddings in Jerusalem are significantly different in many other respects as well and are thus out of the scope of this guide.

## Separating Before the Badeken

For many Ashkenazim and Chassidim, the chosson and kallah do not see each other at all for a full week before the wedding. Even so, some prominent Ashkenaz rabbis suggest that wedding pictures with the chosson and kallah be taken together before the chuppah so as to not to inconvenience the guests; but this rarely happens.

Chabad couples do not even speak on the phone to each other during the week prior to the wedding.

German Jews separate only the day of the wedding, prior to the chuppah.

## Fasting on the Day of the Wedding

It is a widespread custom for the couple to fast on the day of the wedding. One reason is so they do not consume alcohol, which would impair their ability to properly participate in the legal aspects of the wedding.

Sephardim specifically do not fast since the wedding day is similar to a holiday on which fasting would be prohibited.

German Jews do not fast on days that tachnun is not recited, and, in general, are lenient in cases where it is difficult for the chosson or kallah.

## Mikveh

In some communities, the chosson performs ritual immersion in a mikveh on the day of the wedding.

This practice is somewhat different for the kallah, who also performs ritual immersion sometime prior to the wedding. Her immersion is part of the very important framework of the laws of Jewish family purity followed by all religious Jews, the details of which are beyond the scope of this guide.

## Viduy at Mincha

The wedding day represents a new beginning for the young couple and, as a result, their sins are forgiven and they start with a clean slate. In this way, the wedding day is compared to Yom Kippur for the couple. As such, there is a custom for them to pray the Mincha prayers of Yom Kippur on their wedding day. Note that this can take some time and requires planning.

## Part I – Wedding Planning Concepts

### Arev Kablan

In general, an arev kablan is a guarantor who agrees to pay a debt to a creditor in the case of default by a borrower. In regard to weddings, an arev kablan was appointed from each side of the family to cover conditions recorded in the Tenaim. However, due to modern standard forms of the Tenaim document this is not generally done. See section I.1.5, p. 29.

### Prenuptial Agreements

See section I.1.5, p. 29.

### Tenaim

As discussed in section I.1.5, Documentation, tenaim spell out agreements between the families. There are various customs as to when they are done. In the majority of cases, they are executed at the chosson's tisch during the badeken. Some complete them before the wedding, perhaps at the vort. Others do not do them at all.

The mothers of the chosson and kallah typically break a plate after the tenaim are signed and read. This symbolizes the finality of the arrangements: They should not be undone, just as the plate cannot be reconstructed. When and if the tenaim are completed may impact how, when and if the mothers break the plate.

With the advent of Rav Moshe Feinstein's tenaim, some Jews actually dispense with the practice altogether. This is specifically the case regarding German Jews, who often do not read the tenaim at their weddings, and as a result, the mothers do not break a plate.

### Signing the Kethuba

Customs vary as to when the witnesses sign the kethuba. Some have them sign it during the chosson's tisch, while others have them sign it under the chuppah. Sephardim also have the chosson sign the kethuba.

### Badeken

See section I.5.2, p. 70.

### Chuppah in the Sanctuary

Most Ashkenazic and Chassidic Jews specifically avoid conducting the chuppah ceremony in the sanctuary of a shul. However, Sephardim specifically do have the chuppah ceremonies there; and German Jews often do as well.

### Chuppah Outdoors

It is a widespread custom to have the chuppah ceremony outdoors. Some halls have a skylight that opens above the chuppah solely for the purpose of satisfying the outside requirement while keeping the chuppah inside. Note: the chuppah ceremony of a previously married woman is specifically conducted inside.

## Ashes

It is a common custom for Ashkenazim to place a small amount of ashes on the forehead of the chosson just before the chuppah ceremony, in memorial of the destruction of the Temple. This may be done by the father of the chosson or the mesader kiddushin; usually so discreetly that it is rarely noticed.

## Which Way does the Couple Face?

Ashkenazic couples face their guests during the ceremony. But German customs have the couple face away from the guests. At Chabad weddings, the couple faces east. All else being equal, remember the guests who came to share in the simcha and who would want to see the couple as they are getting married.

## Kittel

It is very common for the chosson to wear a kittel under the chuppah. However, there are very many differences as to how he wears it and when he puts it on. Some put it on under the chuppah immediately after arriving. Others put it on earlier. Those who put it on earlier may wear it outside or underneath other clothing.

## Overcoat

A chosson may wear an overcoat during the chuppah ceremony regardless of the temperature in the hall. The main purpose is to hide the kittel for those who do not wear it openly.

## Veil

Veils vary greatly. Some customs, specifically Chassidic, have the kallah wear a very thick veil. If required by custom, then so be it. Otherwise, a very thick veil should be avoided as it looks unnatural and is a tripping hazard for the kallah. I recommend a plain, thin veil or a few layers of thin veils if the kallah wants it thicker. Also, avoid veils with flowers or other patterns as they photograph poorly.

Note that a kallah does not wear a veil if she was previously married.

## Hair

Orthodox Jewish women cover their hair after they are married. But precisely when they start doing so varies widely even within custom communities. Some women may start to cover their hair before the wedding. Others may do so after the chuppah ceremony in the yichud room, while others wait until the entire wedding is over. Check with your rabbi.

Some Chassidic women cut their hair at the wedding as well. Arrangements for this will also have to be made in advance.

The German custom is very particular in that the kallah should cover her hair no later than after entering the yichud room.

*Part I – Wedding Planning Concepts*

## Jewelry

Many kallahs refrain from wearing jewelry under the chuppah. Before the procession, they hand their jewelry to young friends and family members for safe keeping. Holding the jewelry is viewed as a segula for their own simchas.

A related but less common custom is for the couple to loosen shoelaces, belts and other knotted items before the chuppah. This is a Chabad custom, and it is also found among Hungarian Jews.

Incidentally, Chabad has a related custom that the chosson and kallah specifically wear new clothing.

## Candles

It is very common for those escorting the chosson and kallah to the chuppah to carry candles. This is not a typical German custom. However, German Jews do place lit candles on a table near the chuppah.

## Mi Adir

At many weddings, someone sings *Mi Adir* when the chosson arrives under the chuppah. See Blessings 3, p. 130. The German custom is to sing several verses from Hallel. See Blessings 4, p. 130.

## Circling the Chosson

Upon reaching the chuppah, the kallah circles the chosson seven times escorted by the mothers. While circling the chosson, someone sings *Mi Bon Siach*. See Blessings 5, p. 130. This is a well known part of Ashkenazic and Chassidic weddings.

Though not part of the Sephardic or German customs, circling the chosson is often done at those weddings as well.

Whether or not the kallah circles the chosson the German custom is to not sing Mi Bon Siach. The Sephardim sing something but customs vary as to exactly what.

## Tallis

A tallis can find itself a part of the chuppah ceremony in a couple different ways. It might *be* the chuppah being spread over four upright poles. For Sephardim it is draped over the chosson and kallah at some point during the chuppah ceremony. This was also the custom in the Frankfurt region and has since been accepted by most German Jews.

## Reading the Kethuba under the Chuppah

Reading the kethuba under the chuppah is included in the wedding ceremony of all major groups. However, there is a minor difference for Sephardim. The Sephardic kethuba adjures the chosson to keep his responsibilities to his wife with the threat of significant consequences otherwise. To maintain the happiness of the occasion, those passages are not read aloud.

*The Orthodox Jewish Wedding Planner*

## Chosson Oath under the Chuppah

Though the Torah permits a man to have more than one wife, Ashkenazim (including Chassidim and German Jews) have been banned from doing so for over one thousand years by a decree of Rabbenu Gershom. The Sephardim are not bound by that decree, but instead require the chosson to take an oath as part of the chuppah ceremony that he will not take another wife during their marriage.

## Birchas Cohanim under the Chuppah

The Torah directs Cohanim to confer upon the people of Israel a specific blessing. See Blessings 2, p. 129. This blessing is used by others as well, such as when parents bless their children at the Shabbat meal. The Sephardim bestow this blessing upon the chosson and kallah under the chuppah. It is administered either by the mesader kiddushin (whether a Cohen or not) or by a prominent Cohen of the family or community. This is also often done at Chabad weddings, though it is not a specific custom.

## Breaking the Glass

Breaking the glass is ubiquitous among Jewish wedding customs. Most people break the glass as the last event under the chuppah, though a few do it earlier. Breaking the glass is supposed to remind us of the destruction of the Temple and make us aware that we can never achieve perfect happiness until it is rebuilt, may it be speedily in our days.

However, since the breaking of the glass is followed immediately by the joyous dancing of guests escorting the new couple to the yichud room, the mood is somewhat lost. Thus, many people sing *Im Eshkachech*, an excerpt from Psalms 137, to create the proper atmosphere. See Blessings 8, p. 131.

German Jews used to sing Psalm 128 after breaking the glass. See Blessings 9, p. 131. But since pandemonium breaks out so quickly at that point, they now sing it just before breaking the glass.

## Yichud

Generally, Jewish law prohibits a man and woman from enjoying privacy together if they are not married to each other. Entering the yichud room signifies that the newlyweds are fully married according to Jewish law and are permitted privacy. However, even this custom is not universally accepted. Sephardim consider a room in a public hall as falling short of providing true privacy. Rather, the couple satisfies this requirement in their actual home. Thus many Sephardic weddings do not include the rite of yichud at the wedding.

At Chabad weddings, the new couple step over a silver spoon as they enter the yichud room.

## Mezinke Tanz

Ashkenazim have a tradition of honoring parents who marry off their last child with a special dance toward the end of the reception. The parents may be given a wreath of flowers for their heads and decorated brooms. Then the immediate family dances around them while the band plays *Di Mezinke Oysgegebn*. As near as I can tell, mezinke is Yiddish for youngest daughter, but the dance is also done for parents whose last married child is a son.

## *Mitzvah Tanz*

This is a specifically Chassidic custom in which various distinguished people dance with the kallah. The kallah holds one end of a scarf or similar item and the other party holds the other end. The Bostoner Rebbe writes that the chosson dances with the kallah starting with a scarf and finishes dancing hand in hand. See [א], p. 140. This is not a Chabad custom, and decidedly is not done in other communities.

# I.1.5 Documentation✓

Several legal documents must be acquired and prepared for the wedding. It is critical that they be prepared in advance.

## *Kethuba*

The kethuba is the main Jewish wedding document. It is written in Aramaic and defines the responsibilities of the husband to the wife. Many couples purchase an ornate, custom kethuba to decorate their home. Some prefer not to do this for two reasons. First, the text of the kethuba is not all that romantic but rather technical, including the husband's responsibilities in the case of divorce or in the event that he predeceases his wife. Second, since the kethuba is the wife's proof to certain rights, ideally it should remain secured and out of sight.

In any case, the mesader kiddushin should have standard forms. They can also be purchased at Jewish bookstores. Wherever you get it, consult with the mesader kiddushin to determine how much of it can be completed beforehand, and how much must be left blank until the wedding. Also note that several circumstances may require special wording in the kethuba. A second marriage is one example.

## *Tenaim*

Long ago, families would agree to various stipulations regarding the support of the new couple. These stipulations would be recorded in tenaim (literally, conditions). Today, we use a standard tenaim form promulgated by Rav Moshe Feinstein zt''l, which basically states that all parties agree that all conditions have already been satisfied and that neither family has any claim against the other which would interfere with proceeding with the wedding.

## *Prenuptial Agreements*

A recent trend in Orthodox marriages is to execute prenuptial agreements (pre-nups) before the wedding. They are intended to protect the husband and wife from legal tangles that could arise from a divorce. Specifically, if the couple was to get a civil divorce and the husband refused to grant his wife a Jewish divorce or the wife refused to accept a Jewish

---

✓ See Checklist 20 – Documentation, page 107.

divorce from the husband, the other party would not be able to remarry under Jewish law. The pre-nups are designed to pressure the other party to properly terminate the marriage according to Jewish law.

There is a good deal of controversy surrounding pre-nups. Some Orthodox rabbis will not officiate at weddings that use them. Other Orthodox rabbis will not officiate at weddings that *don't* use them. Likewise, some families insist on them, while other families insist they not be used. Thus, from a planning perspective, these issues must be addressed. The worst possible scenario would be to wait until the wedding day to discover that everyone's opinions are at odds with each other.

## *Shtar Chalitza*

In a similar vein, I have seen mention of a shtar chalitza (document of release), which the brothers of the chosson sign. This obligates them to perform the rite of release from Levirate marriage should the chosson pass away leaving no descendents. See Deuteronomy 25:5-9. However, it seems that this document is not executed nowadays.

## *Marriage License*

Most Jewish weddings are a combination of a religious and civil ceremony. To be duly married, the couple must register and fulfill several requirements of the state. Most states have a Web site with specific information. Other, third-party Web sites list information for all states, but it is better to go directly to the source. Some requirements may be:

- Proof of age
- Parental consent if either one of the couple is younger than 18 years old
- Proof of identity
- Blood test results
- Processing fees
- Waiting period after filing the license
- Various proofs regarding the disposition of previous marriages
- Residency requirements
- Witnesses
- An officiant who is registered with the state
- Marriage courses

The license should be obtained in a timely manner in the jurisdiction (city or county) of the *location of the wedding* – *not* the jurisdiction of the residence of the chosson or kallah. It is not legal to perform a wedding without the proper licensing, and many rabbis will refuse to do so if a valid marriage license is not present at the ceremony. Though many rabbis are registered with their local state some may not be. In any case, the rabbi (or someone representative) must be registered in the state of the location of the wedding.

After the marriage, the license is returned to the government for official recording, and then a marriage certificate may be issued to the couple (which may involve an additional fee).

When the wedding is out of town and obtaining a license is difficult, some couples have a civil marriage locally followed by the Jewish marriage later. In this case, the Jewish wedding is purely a religious ceremony with no secular legal significance. The rabbi should be consulted to be sure that the civil procedure does not cause any Jewish legal problems. In this case, the marriage certificate should be brought to the wedding to attest to compliance with all secular legal requirements.

## I.2 Selecting Vendors✓

Many people and organizations will be providing support during the wedding. Here are a few general considerations that are more or less common among all of them. I will refer to them as the vendor basics throughout the rest of this guide.

### *Availability*

⚠ It may seem obvious that your vendors must be available on the day of the wedding to provide services, but sometimes "available" is not what you think it is. For instance, you could book a band and discover on the wedding day that the lead singer didn't show up due to another engagement and instead provided a stand-in. Similarly, the caterer may have several affairs that day and might supply a less-experienced manager to service your event. This can be true also for the photographer and others. Be clear as to exactly who will be servicing your wedding on the wedding day, and specify this explicitly in the contract.

### *Orthodox Jewish Wedding Experience*

Orthodox Jewish weddings are complicated events with activities occurring in many places in quick succession. But they also flow in a predictable pattern. Those familiar with this are better prepared to support you. Those who are not will have to be instructed and coached.

### *Longevity*

There is no guarantee that a business you contract with today will be around tomorrow to provide the agreed-upon services. However, well-established businesses are more reliable. Given a choice, choose one that has been around for several years.

### *References*

References are important to help determine how likely a vendor is to deliver that which they claim. You may ask the vendor or find your own references if you have friends who have made weddings in your area.

### *Points of Contact*

Be sure you know how to get in touch with your vendors quickly and reliably. Get a cell phone number if you can. For a larger organization, be sure you have direct access to a single person who can be relied upon for consultation and assistance.

Enter contact information into Checklist 24 – Participants, p. 119.

### *Cancellation Policies*

Find out how much of a deposit is required, what the refund policy is on deposits and what the cancellation policies are.

---

✓ These items are included in each of the vendor selection checklists.

## Using the Checklists

The vendor selection checklists at the end of the guide are useful for comparing the information you get from various vendors. However, vendors may not appreciate being interrogated with a long list of questions. Better would be to ask for a written proposal or to meet with each vendor casually and then call the vendor afterwards to fill in the missing pieces.

## Contract

Make sure you get a written, signed contract from the vendor that specifies all of the details. Most vendors will be more eager than you are to finalize the deal with a signed contract. Just be sure that all details are accounted for.

Like all of the recommendations in this guide, these are not absolute. For instance, if you are willing to accept a vendor with less experience, then you may be able to negotiate a better price. It depends on how comfortable you are with the vendor's ability to provide the needed services.

*The Orthodox Jewish Wedding Planner*

## I.2.1 Selecting a Hall[✓]

Once the date has been set, the next step is to book the hall. If no hall is available for your selected date, you will have to choose another date. Do this soon. The longer you wait, the slimmer your chances of finding a hall on the desired date. This is especially true if you have selected a weekend or holiday. Solidifying the hall facilitates many of the other arrangements.

Photo 2 – Bais Faiga - Lakewood, New Jersey

When looking for a hall, refer to the vendor basics from section I.2. Of considerable importance are clear points of contact for both contractual issues before the wedding and facility issues on the day of the wedding.

Also consider
- Price — Is it within your budget?
- Location — Is it easy to get to?
- Size — Is it right for the number of guests (not too big or too small)?
- Layout — Can it accommodate all of the wedding activities?
- Ambience — Is it fitting for a Jewish wedding?
- Caterers — How does the hall work with caterers?

### *Types of Halls*

What is a hall? Basically, it is any facility with the resources and inclination to host a wedding. Some examples are:
- Commercial halls
- Synagogues
- Hotels
- Schools
- Golf / Country Clubs
- Museums
- Arboretums, Topiary Gardens

Be careful about getting too creative. Setting up a kosher affair in an unusual environment could be expensive.

---

[✓] See Checklist 7 – Selecting a Hall, page 86.

*Part I – Wedding Planning Concepts*

## Price

Price essentially depends on the number of guests and the facilities you need. There is no end to the list of supplemental charges a hall can tack on, so get a list of all of them. Here are some additional charges to look for:
- Cleaning fees
- Chair/table/stands setup and rental fees
    - This can add up. For example, if you need to reconfigure a chuppah room into a dining room, someone will have to do the actual moving, and that someone will want to be paid.
    - Platforms for the chuppah and the band
- Fees for the use of extra rooms
- Liquor/soda fees (even if you are supplying your own liquor)
- Coatroom service (which you may or may not need)
- Parking
- Cancellation Policy

The price covers the use of the hall for a certain period of time. Find out how much time the contract includes and the charge for additional time. A typical wedding takes about five hours to set up and lasts for about five hours.

## Location

Several things make one hall location better than another. Check these factors:
- Is it easy to get to?
- Does it have ample parking?
- Is it in a safe neighborhood?
- Is it out of the way of other attractions, such as large sports facilities that could cause traffic problems?
- Is it near lodging facilities for out-of-town guests?

## Size and Layout

Layout is very important. Unlike many non-Jewish weddings which require only a single reception room, Jewish weddings use a lot of space. If the hall is not familiar with Jewish weddings, let them know what you will need. Consider where the various phases of the wedding will be staged. Specifically, see that there is room for:
- The kallah's preparation area
- The chosson's preparation area
- The badeken
- The chosson's tisch
- The chuppah
- The yichud room
- The family photography area
- The banquet area
- The dance floor

*The Orthodox Jewish Wedding Planner*

Each of these areas must provide sufficient space, including easy access from one to the other. One large area may be divided into several smaller spaces; and some areas may serve multiple functions. However, sharing functions should be planned carefully so as not to cause a significant disturbance to the flow of activities. As you look at a hall, think of how the event will unfold. In particular, be sure that there is enough room for a large group of men to escort the chosson to the kallah for the badeken. Similarly, consider how the procession will flow to the chuppah. There should be a well-defined center aisle. Lastly, imagine how the chosson and kallah will enter the dance area during the meal. For example, they shouldn't have to navigate through a long row of tables. I have seen several halls lacking one or more of these three essential features.

**Photo 3 – Badeken       - Escorting the Chosson to the Kallah**

**Photo 4 – Center Aisle Leading to Chuppah**

*Part I – Wedding Planning Concepts*

Photo 5 – New Couple's Grand Entrance

The hall should also have a lobby that provides easy access to all of the areas described above. It should also present a well-defined entrance, including a place to hang coats, and permit guests to use restrooms and find seating cards.

Using one of the preparation rooms for a yichud room can be done with minimal disturbance. Similarly, if the chosson's tisch and badeken areas are in the dining room and dance area, they can be converted during the chuppah ceremony. The longest delays occur when the chuppah area is used for something else, since most activities come either right before or right after the chuppah ceremony. An exception may be formal family pictures, which should take minimal time to set up and may benefit from using the chuppah.

Depending on custom and preference, you may want the chuppah ceremony outdoors or in the sanctuary. Verify that the hall can suit your needs. See section I.1.4, p. 23.

💡 When deciding where to place the chuppah, try to leave about two feet behind it. This will allow photographers and others to move from side to side during the chuppah ceremony with minimum distraction to the guests.

You will also need ample room on the sides of the chuppah if you expect procession members to stay by the chuppah during the ceremony. You will also need space to the right of the chuppah for those honored with a blessing under the chuppah since they typically remain there until the end of the ceremony.

Consider an elevated platform for the chuppah. This will help the guests get a better view of the proceedings. It will also reduce the number of people who will crowd around the chuppah to take pictures. This may be a good or bad thing depending on how many pictures you want from friends and relatives. However, also consider the extra difficulty a raised platform could present for honorees who may have trouble negotiating steps.

## Support Staff

Ask the hall what support staff will be on duty on the wedding day. Will someone be available in the event of facility problems such as lighting, heating and air conditioning? Will housekeeping services be available if needed?

## Ambience

Ambience encompasses several aspects. The most obvious are general aesthetics such as:
- Cleanliness
- State of repair
- Lighting

Lighting is important. Some halls wish to promote a romantic atmosphere with dim lights. This creates a significant problem for photographers. In such situations, seasoned photographers will bring their own lighting, destroy the romantic atmosphere and get great pictures.

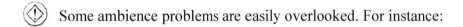 Some ambience problems are easily overlooked. For instance:

- Is the hall decorated with inappropriate statues and/or paintings?
- Is it near a large source of noise such as a major roadway, railroad or factory?
- If you are going to have an outdoor chuppah, is there a suitable place for it? You don't want the chuppah out back by the dumpsters.
- Will you have exclusive use of the hall and all accompanying rooms and lobbies? Other concurrent activities may be distracting to your event. In certain venues, such as hotels, you should expect other patrons to be milling about. In others, such as banquet halls, no one else should be around. In yet others, such as schools, community centers and synagogues, you may or may not be provided with exclusive use.

## Caterers

Ask if the hall works solely with specific caterers, or prefers certain caterers to others. Also ask if the hall typically negotiates with the caterer rather than directly with the customer.

## Security

While your mind is on the young couple, relatives, friends and all of the people who will be helping you pull off this wedding, you are probably not thinking of the bad guys. But they

are thinking about you! The extent of this problem depends on the venue. Ask the hall about security issues such as:
- Are security measures in force?
    - Cameras
    - Patrols
- Are facilities available to secure valuables such as gifts and clothing?

## Details

Find out if the hall provides specific Jewish wedding needs. This may not be the deciding factor between one hall and another, but once you have decided on a hall you will need to know if it gives you certain things or if you will have to get them from somewhere else.
- Chuppah
- Kallah's chair
- Sound system
- Elevated platforms for chuppah and badeken

## After Choosing a Hall

Make sure you have contact numbers of individuals to call for any questions concerning the hall rental. Also, be sure you know who will be on duty the day of the wedding to address any concerns that may arise at that time.

*The Orthodox Jewish Wedding Planner*

## I.2.2 Selecting a Caterer✓

Once the hall has been set, you can choose a caterer. This is the typical order of things. However, some mitigating factors may cause you to change the hall. For instance, some caterers may only service certain halls. Likewise, some halls may have exclusive deals with certain caterers.

Check the vendor basics (section I.2, p. 32). The caterer is one of the most important vendors of the wedding, so choose well.

For a religious Jewish wedding you want to be sure that the caterer has the highest standards of kosher supervision. Many of your guests will trust that you have made certain that this is true. Ask the caterer to identify the kosher-supervision agency, and then verify this independently with that agency.

**Photo 6 – Watermelon Swans**

The basic price should include one meal per guest. In addition, you may want a smorgasbord or refreshments for events earlier in the wedding. Note that the caterer may give you a basic price and assume you know that there are additional expenses, such as:
- Mashgiach fees
- Kashering fees – The kitchen in the hall will most likely need to be cleaned and kashered before use.
- Liquor
- Extra setup fees for things like
    - Wine service
    - Dessert service
- Meals for the orchestra members, photographers and other assistants

Ask the caterer to give you a total price including all fees.

($) Note that your caterer may be able to negotiate a complete package deal for you that includes the hall fees. This may save money since the caterer can anticipate unexpected hall fees and may have a better bargaining position with the hall than you do.

---

✓ See Checklist 8 – Selecting a Caterer, page 89.

## *Menu*

Make sure that the caterer provides high quality food. Personally, I cannot distinguish between filet mignon and shoe leather. But if you can, ask to taste menu samples to help decide between menu options. A caterer may not have as many options as a typical restaurant, but should offer several choices to accommodate both price and taste.

Most caterers provide alternate meal options for guests with various dietary restrictions or preferences. Check that they can supply fish, vegetarian and other special meals.

### Buffet or Served

Many weddings are served buffet style. Surprisingly, a buffet may not cost any less per person than a formally served meal. Typically, the trade-off is between the more formal atmosphere of a served meal and the more food choices of a buffet. You may want to have part of the meal served by waiters and another part set up as a buffet, such as the salad or desserts.

## *Special Requests*

In an unending effort to be unique, caterers continually bring new food offerings to weddings. Some may add to the simcha, others simply add to the cost, while yet others may be ill-advised.

### Ceremonial Challah

You may want a large challah for the chosson and kallah at the meal. Some people look forward to getting a piece of this challah as a segula for various blessings. Remember, however, that the guests should have their own rolls and thus may not consume much of a large challah.

### Chocolate Fountain

 A now-common specialty is a chocolate fountain. Though tempting, weigh the joy of chocolate-covered strawberries in the gleeful hands of chocolate-covered children, against the angst of their parents.

### Mini Burgers

Miniature hamburgers on indoor grills sometimes pop up at weddings. Unless the wedding atmosphere is decidedly casual, these mini barbecues may seem out of place.

### Water

An outside chuppah could expose your guests to a lot of sun and heat. If so, ask the caterer to provide plenty of small, chilled water bottles.

### More Stuff

Other specialty items such as fruit sculptures and punch fountains can add to your cost, but otherwise fit well with the wedding atmosphere.

## Chuppah Support

Ask the caterer if he/she supplies some of the items needed for the wedding such as:
- Wine and glasses for sheva brachos under the chuppah and after the meal
- Special chairs for the chosson and kallah
- Chuppah
- Mechitza

## The Yichud Room

Remember that the chosson and kallah may not have eaten all day and will be very hungry by the time they reach the yichud room. Make sure food is provided for them. Eating and drinking in the yichud room also have special religious significance, as dining together alone is an important marriage activity. Also, discuss any special requests the chosson and kallah might have with the caterer.

Sometimes, friends may want to prepare food for the couple for various sentimental reasons. This practice should be discouraged as it can cause problems for the caterer who must adhere to strict kosher rules regarding any food that enters the hall during the affair.

## Crashers

If the chosson or kallah has a large contingent of friends, they may show up uninvited to share in the simcha. This is usually a good thing, since the enthusiasm of the young couple's friends is very uplifting.

Usually, they will not expect to be seated at a full formal meal with the other guests, and you may be able to make less costly arrangements for them. The caterer should be able to assist you with this.

If you are planning to place large platters of food on tables for the crashers to help themselves, the food should be served after the seated guests are served their main course. Alternatively, it may be served in another room. Either way, the seated guests should not think that they are being offered another smorgasbord.

## Alternate Dinner Arrangements

The standard dining arrangement at a Jewish wedding includes some refreshments prior to the badeken (ranging from light snacks to an elaborate smorgasbord), followed by a formal meal after the chuppah ceremony. Some sort of formal meal is essential since a wedding requires a "mitzvah meal." However, this could be prohibitively expensive for those with many more friends than they can afford to feed. The following are alternatives that I have seen. None are ideal; each has its pros and cons. But one may suit your situation more than another. Refer to Figure 1, p. 44.

*Part I – Wedding Planning Concepts*

### Option 1 – Chuppah Only

This is one of the more common options. Some guests are invited to the chuppah ceremony and then leave. The drawback is that fewer people are around for the dancing. All other options try to address this problem.

### Option 2 – First Dance Only

This option invites some guests to stay through the first dance. Refreshments are provided to these guests while the other guests are seated for a full meal. This has several drawbacks. First, the seated guests may not understand that the refreshments are only for the non-seated guests. Second, the seated guests are sitting, eating appetizers while the non-seated guests are standing. Third, the point at which the non-seated guests leave is not as clear as in option 1.

### Option 3 – Come Back for Dessert

Another option is to invite some of the guests back for the last dance and dessert. This has the benefit of allowing these guests to participate in the sheva brachos after the meal. However this also has some problems. First, very few guests will take the trouble to come back to the hall once they have left. Second, if the timing is not precise, those coming back for dessert may return in the middle of the meal.

### Option 4 – Meal Last

In this option, no meal is served until all the dancing is over. Refreshments are served during the dancing, which will add to the cost, but the final meal may have very few people and be much less expensive. The entire wedding, from beginning to end, may be longer, but some time is saved during the dancing since no meal is served in the middle.

### Option 5 – Simpler Meal

Here, you invite everyone to everything. You save money by providing a simpler meal. This may appeal to those who find the two-class feature of the other options distasteful. However, it may be difficult to reduce the price of the meals.

*The Orthodox Jewish Wedding Planner*

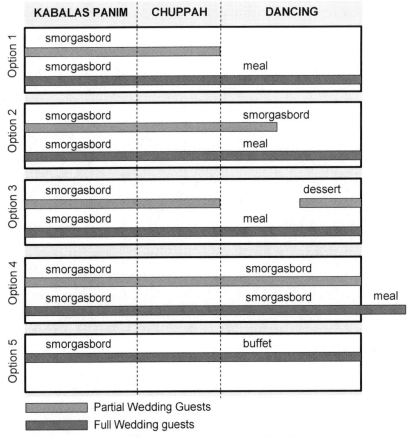

Figure 1 – Meal Arrangement Options

In all cases, send a response card as part of the invitation to those guests invited to the meal. Send the other guests response cards only if you need a precise count as to how many are coming. For example, in option 1, the number of guests attending only the chuppah changes the price minimally, if at all. In this case response cards are not sent to those not invited to the meal. However, regardless of which option you choose, some guests may not understand and, once at the chuppah, may assume that they are invited to the meal as well. There should only be a small number of them, and you might simply want to be prepared to seat a few extra guests if this occurs.

## Table Décor

Your caterer should be able to provide a variety of colors for the tablecloths and napkins. Make sure you see samples as the color names may not accurately describe their actual appearance. Your caterer may also be able to supply centerpieces at a much lower cost than a florist. Some communities have gemachs that supply these as well.

## Wedding Cake

A formal wedding cake is not an essential feature of a Jewish wedding. If you want one, be sure to discuss it with the caterer. He/she may be able to provide it for you, or you may have to procure it elsewhere. Keep in mind that the caterer will most likely serve some other dessert, and the new couple may find themselves eating frozen wedding cake for many months after the wedding.

## Layout

Discuss details of the layout and progression of the wedding with the caterer. This should include which rooms will be used for what. Remember to minimize the amount of time guests have to stand around waiting for rooms to be converted from one use to another. If you must rearrange rooms during the wedding, have helpers direct your guests accordingly.

## Schedule

Discuss the wedding schedule with the caterer. Experienced caterers will know what to do when. Those caterers who have not done many weddings need to plan carefully. For example, it is usually advisable to have the guests served first at the meal before the family, since the family will be taking pictures. Let the caterer know where family members will be seated.

Frequently, a caterer driven by efficiency will be overzealous in clearing portions from the tables before the guests can eat them. Instruct the caterer to allow the guests sufficient time before clearing plates.

## Liquor

If you follow the FLOP method of dividing expenses, then liquor is funded by the chosson's family. Nonetheless, it may actually be provided by the caterer or the hall, which are typically the responsibility of the kallah's family. In this instance, there must be a good deal of cooperation between the families since one side may be selecting a hall or caterer from which the other side will be obligated to buy the liquor. If the liquor does not come from the caterer, be certain it is approved by the mashgiach.

☺ In my opinion, there should be as little liquor at a wedding as possible. First, liquor at a wedding quickly finds its way into the hands of young people, which is both illegal and dangerous. Even if caterers pledge to card everyone they serve, they rarely do. And even if they do, older guests will often pass drinks to the younger ones. Second, a wedding is not only a very festive affair, but also a very spiritual occasion. People acting beneath their normal dignity can have a significant negative impact on the entire event. An open bar is asking for trouble. Even a simple bottle of wine at each adult table can end up in the wrong hands. A wine service, where waiters pour only one or two glasses to every adult guest, is a more reasonable solution.

## Staff

The caterer will have far more people supporting your event than any other vendor. Ask the caterer about the size of his support staff. Also impress on him/her that you expect the staff to act professionally and courteously toward your guests. Experienced catering staff members are typically friendly and accommodating, but even the best caterers can have an occasional grouch who can quickly foul the mood.

## Excess Food

Find out what is done with excess food from the wedding. Food that has been served cannot be salvaged but there may be other leftovers. The caterer may be able to contact a charitable organization that can use the surplus food to feed the less fortunate.

## I.2.3 Selecting a Florist✓

Nothing at a wedding has a wider price range than flowers. I have been to weddings with *no* flowers other than the bridal bouquet. I have been to weddings where the kallah had only a single rose. Total flower bill: $1.98.

If you have access to a flower gemach, you may be able to get a large quantity of silk flowers for a fraction of the price of fresh flowers.

If you are selecting a florist, remember the vendor basics mentioned in section I.2 p. 32. Experience with Jewish weddings is not as critical here since flower placement is straightforward. The only exception is that some florists might be able to provide a chuppah whereas others may not.

### *Flower Arrangements*

Flowers can go everywhere, but typically, they are placed in several key locations. By asking the florist to break down the price by location, you can better understand what you are paying for. Standard floral arrangements are:
- The bridal bouquet
- Corsages, boutonnières and bouquets for family members
- Decorating the badeken
- Decorating the chuppah
- Table settings
- The mechitza
- Arrangements in the lobby

Note that the badeken flowers can be moved to the chuppah and then again to the dining room.

The most elaborate floral arrangements surround the chuppah and decorate the tables. The chuppah decorations can (but do not have to) include flowers on the chuppah poles, arrangements on pedestals down the aisle (let's see how many get knocked over), and assorted arrangements around the chuppah area.

There is no limit to how elaborate table arrangements can be. But there is also no limit to how creative *you* can be to make arrangements that are elegant and inexpensive. Here are some alternatives:

---

✓ See Checklist 9 – Selecting a Florist, page 91.

- Some organizations provide decorated gift baskets to support charity.
- With simple things like mirrored tiles and candles, you can make very nice centerpieces yourself.
- With separate seating, simpler arrangements can be made for the men's side.

## Down the Aisle

☺ A runner (usually paper) is a common decoration down the aisle. This is a *bad* idea for two reasons. First, many guests will trample it well before the chosson and kallah ever set foot on it. Second, it quickly wrinkles and becomes a tripping hazard. Some florists, with varying success, tie a ribbon across the end of the runner to discourage people from walking down the aisle.

💡 Placing tulle down the sides of the aisle for the first few rows looks very nice and may be very useful. For example, it may prevent some of your amateur photographer guests from obscuring the view of the paid photographers during the procession. On the other hand, be sure someone removes it prior to the end of the chuppah so friends can come to dance the chosson and kallah to the yichud room. See Photo 4, p. 36.

If you are having elaborate floral arrangements, be sure that the florist will remain until the end of the chuppah to attend to any mishaps. Note also that all of this flora will reside in various vases and pots. Be sure you are clear as to what has to be returned to the florist and how it will get there.

## After the Wedding

Ask the florist for suggestions about how to dispose of the flowers. One idea is to send them to various nursing homes and hospitals around town.

## I.2.4 Selecting an Orchestra✓

Choosing an orchestra is simple from a planning perspective. It is mostly a matter of taste and budget. Again look for the vendor basics discussed in section I.2, p. 32. Here, Jewish wedding experience is very important since the orchestra needs to be in the right place at the right time playing the right music. Remember too that not all music is appropriate for a Jewish wedding. Some orchestras might not be familiar with basic issues such as restrictions on women's voices, inappropriate subject matter and mixed dancing.

Checking availability is most important since an orchestra is more likely than other vendors to provide substitutes. If you are particular about a certain individual, specify in the contract that his presence is required.

☺ It is my opinion that every orchestra plays way too loudly. Even the dinner music is typically so loud that guests cannot easily socialize. Not only is it irritating, but elevated music volumes can actually cause permanent hearing damage. Also, musical quality suffers as the volume increases to the point where all orchestras sound the same. This is one place where paying more gets you less.

$ Consider a one-man band. He can combine talent and technology to produce beautiful wedding music at a fraction of the price of a larger group. Again, be careful of the volume. Some one-man bands increase their volume unnecessarily to compensate for being only one person, sometimes to the point of being louder than larger bands.

A disc jockey is another option, but it is not common and might not save much money. Also, few disc jockeys are familiar with religious sensitivities regarding mixed dancing and inappropriate music.

Sometimes family members, friends or even the chosson may want to perform a special song. If this is the case, be sure that the orchestra can and will cooperate. It seems simple, but licensing restrictions and other issues might present unexpected obstacles.

A few things you will want to ask the orchestra are:
- Do they know how to play the couple's favorite songs?
- Do they have sound samples?
- Do they play during all phases of the wedding?

---

✓ See Checklist 10 – Selecting an Orchestra, page 93.

- Can they provide special instrumentation? Perhaps you would like a flute, harp or banjo. If so, make your requests known up front.
- Are they sensitive to excessive volume?

Get the total price. Some things that may cost extra are:
- Bandstand (might be provided by the hall)
- Amplification equipment (including extra microphones)
- Sound technician
- Setup
- Overtime

Someone, usually the chosson and kallah, will have to meet with the orchestra leader to coordinate the music for the various phases of the wedding, especially the processional.

## I.2.5 Selecting a Photographer✓

Photographic tastes are very personal, and it may be difficult to find someone who sees the world just as you do. But in any case, a few general tips will make the photographic part of the wedding run smoother. Remember the vendor basics (section I.2, p. 32), especially having Orthodox Jewish wedding experience. With so much going on simultaneously, you'll want a photographer who can capture as much of it as possible.

### *Digital versus Film*

Digital photography is certainly the modern trend. But, some photographers prefer film because it delivers higher quality photographs. On the other hand, it does not allow the photographer to view shots immediately and may be more expensive. Note also that it is much easier to correct minor errors in digital photos.

If you have a preference, be sure that the photographer is equipped and willing to comply.

### *Business Considerations*

Several business practices may lead you to prefer one photographer over another. For instance, does the photographer deliver only prints or will he also provide the original negatives and/or digital images? Also, what copyrights, if any, apply?

Get a sense of how long the photographer requires to produce the final product. I know of couples who had children well before seeing their wedding photos.

Similarly, be clear as to how many photos are included in the main album and what arrangements should be made for parent albums.

 Let the photographer know that images from your wedding may not be used in any advertising without your explicit consent.

### **Crew**

It may be advantageous to have at least two photographers since often two things are happening at once during the wedding. For example, the kallah makes her grand entrance into the badeken room while several things are happening at the chosson's tisch. Also, since men and women dance on different sides of the mechitza, it helps to have one photographer on each side.

---

✓ See Checklist 11 – Selecting a Photographer, page 95; Checklist 12 – Selecting a Videographer, page 97; and Checklist 13 – Poses, page 98.

Without this, a good photographer will make do. For instance, he/she will typically bring a ladder to set up between the dance areas to be able to take pictures of both sides.

### Lighting

Ambient lighting in wedding halls is often grossly insufficient for wedding photography. Ask the photographer if he will be bringing supplemental lighting. If so, you will have much better pictures.

## *Photographic Interaction*

In some respects, photography is one of the more important aspects of the event since it creates a lasting record. However, you need to balance the benefit of capturing the moment with the inevitable interference it will cause. The following are issues to consider. There is no right or wrong here; it will depend solely upon your personal preference.

### Studio Time

Weddings take months to plan and hours to happen. You will not want to consume those few hours taking lots of photos. People often schedule separate family photos prior to the wedding. However, you need to consider how many of those photos you will actually want. Typically, the most important pictures include the chosson and kallah together. Ask yourself if you would want to purchase an 8x10 glossy of the parents and the kallah alone or the parents and the chosson alone to display on the mantle. If not, don't waste time taking these pictures.

Likewise, photographers take lots of pictures with the kallah or chosson and individual siblings. Sometimes they will experiment with comical poses. Most of this simply wastes time generating photos that you will never purchase.

The bottom line is that you have to take the majority of the posed wedding photos after the chuppah, just at the point where you would rather be dancing with the guests. Since this is the case, you need a photographer who is organized and fast. It might help to list the posed pictures that you want taken beforehand and give it to the photographer. See Checklist 13 – Poses, p. 106.

### In Your Face

In order to get the absolutely best pictures, the photographers must have the best view, usually to the exclusion of everyone else. Unless you specify otherwise, expect them to be under the chuppah between the chosson and kallah and pushing the parents aside.

Some photographers demand a replay of every stunt during the dancing so that they can capture it on film. Again, this may make for pretty pictures but can seriously impinge on the spontaneity and enjoyment of the wedding. Let the photographer know your preference.

### Videography

In addition to still photos, you may want to hire someone to produce a video recording of the wedding. Here are some things to consider.

A photographer with a videographer on staff will provide several benefits. First, the package deal may cost less than separate services. Second, their activities will be coordinated with less chance of mutual interference.

⚖️ The nature of the final package is just as important here as it is with still pictures. If the video you receive will be largely unedited, then it will probably be long and tedious to watch. On the other hand, a well-edited video requires a lot of effort and could be very expensive.

Find out what the final format will be. Most videographers now produce a DVD, though some may still use VHS.

The "In Your Face" concerns with still photographers apply even more so to videographers. Many have a tendency to close in on each guest and ask them to say something impromptu into the camera. Some guests like this, while others may find it very disturbing.

Even if you personally don't enjoy watching videos (like me), they may be very much appreciated by family members who missed the wedding – especially those who were too ill to attend.

## Separate Dancing

Separate dancing is a hallmark of religious weddings. It testifies to the importance of modest behavior between men and women. This becomes an issue with male photographers trying to record events occurring on the women's side of the dance floor. The degree of sensitivity and the solutions depend upon the parties involved, so this should be thought out in advance.

At one end of the spectrum, women may wish to avoid men watching them dance at all and may not want any record of it either. Short of that, you may prefer a female photographer who can easily maneuver among the women while another, male photographer works the men's side.

Without a female photographer, an experienced male photographer will be able to take great photos while staying out of the way. But in this case, it would be advisable to remind the photographer to give the women plenty of room.

# I.3 Guests✓

The emotional enthusiasm and participation of the guests contribute more to the atmosphere of the wedding than all of the outward trappings. Organizing the list of guests is probably the most difficult task. Doing this job well will greatly increase the success of your simcha.

## Whom to Invite

This is a very difficult question, one which each family will have to struggle with based on the scope of the wedding. One practical decision is whether or not to invite some guests to the entire affair (including the meal) and other guests only to the chuppah ceremony (and perhaps dancing). See Alternate Dinner Arrangements, p.42. Again, this is a tough choice, but once it is made, tracking is straightforward.

## I.3.1 Tracking Guests

### Data Integrity

A list of all guests must be compiled and maintained. This list is critical as it will guide many additional activities. This data is only as good as it is accurate. The first step to assuring data accuracy is to have only one authentic copy. Someone, typically the parents of the kallah, should keep the one and only official copy of the guest list. Copies should be made for backup and to give to others who need working copies, but only one version should be the master copy.

### Data Media

You can keep the data anywhere. You can organize it on note cards, spiral-bound notebooks or even sticky notes. However, using a software program will have many advantages, such as:
- It is easy to change. There will be many changes in the guest list as you change your mind or add those whom you may have forgotten. Any data system must be flexible to changes.
- It is easy to sort.
- It can automate other tasks such as creating mailing labels and seating cards.
- It is easy to distribute via email.
- It is easy to back up by copying the data file to another computer or drive.
- You may be able to do simple calculations such as the total number of expected guests.

There are several wedding-planning software packages that maintain guest lists electronically. I have never used any of them since I find simple spreadsheets to be easy, flexible and adequate. The more you know how to use spreadsheets, the more they will

---

✓ See Checklist 14 – Guest List Sample, page 100, and

Checklist 15 – Seating List Sample, page 102.

help you in organizing a wedding. Complicated uses of spreadsheet programs are beyond the scope of this guide. Here we will discuss some simple table setups that should provide a lot of benefit with little effort.

## *Basic Data Organization*

Essentially, you need two data tables: one to track the invitations and another to track the seating arrangements.

### Invitation Data Table

An example of a data table to track invitations is given in Checklist 14, p. 108. Each row of this table represents a single, mailed invitation.

As shown in the example, the table should have enough information to fully address each invitation and track how many guests are expected and which have responded.

If you sum up the number of guests to count how many meals you will need, remember to include support people who do not get invitations but do get meals.
- Photographers
- Orchestra members
- Babysitters
- Ushers
- Chosson and kallah, parents and at-home siblings

You can add these as rows in the invitation table, but don't fill in the address information and don't send them invitations.

It is important to realize that this table will be very dynamic. You will start with some initial information, which you will have to update as more becomes available.

### Seating Assignment Data Table

This data table will be critical before and during the wedding. It will track who is sitting where, and which special meals have been requested. In this table, each row represents a single seating card. For separate seating, each person will have his/her own card. For family seating, you may want to have a single card for a couple or a family. See Checklist 15, p. 110.

If you build this data table in a spreadsheet program, you will be able to sort it either by table number or last name. You will need the seating list sorted both ways at the wedding. If a seating card is lost, the sorted-by-name list will help you quickly find where the person should be. If someone not previously assigned a seat needs to be seated at the last minute, the sorted-by-table list will help you find an appropriate place. You can also extract a list of the special meal requests for use by the caterer.

*The Orthodox Jewish Wedding Planner*

**Other Seating Arrangements**

Not everyone prepares detailed seating assignments for the wedding meal. In some Chassidic circles, no seats are assigned at all. People sit wherever they like. Others have signs on the tables that identify groups of people alone. For example, one table may say "Friends of the Cohens from Shul."

Such lackadaisical planning makes check-box-hugging people like me squeamish. But if you are inclined to do this, consider the following. Will guests want to sit in large groups? If families will be sitting together, especially parents with children, then awkward situations could arise if large groups of seats are not available for them. On the other hand, if you will be having separate seating with most people sitting as individuals, then this will be less of a problem. With planned seating, you can set almost exactly the proper number of seats with only a few extras for last-minute changes. But for free-roaming seating, you should plan to have many more seats then you have guests since random seating will use the resources much less efficiently.

## *Keep the Data*

Be sure to save the address information after the wedding. You will need it for mailing thank-you notes and, G-d willing, for future simchas.

*Part I – Wedding Planning Concepts*

# I.3.2 Invitations✓

Now that you know whom you'd like to invite, you have to let them know by sending invitations. Your guest list does not have to be done at this point; just complete enough to give you an idea as to how many invitations to buy. Basically, the style of the invitations will depend on your personal taste and budget. But there are some issues to consider from a planning perspective.

Timing can be worked out in reverse. Ask your guests to respond about four weeks prior to the wedding. Don't give them too much time to respond as they might forget. Allow two additional weeks for mailing and delivery.

Give yourself another week to address and stamp the envelopes. This means you have to have the invitations, in hand, seven weeks prior to the wedding. Most invitation vendors can produce invitations within two weeks. But it will probably take at least a week to decide on the style and to perfect the wording.

The bottom line is, in the best case scenario, you should decide on an invitation vendor and start the selection process at least ten weeks prior to the wedding. See Checklist 2, p. 88.

## *Selecting a Vendor*

The vendor basics (section I.2, p. 32) apply here as well. Experience can be particularly helpful when trying to select the appropriate wording.

💡 Many vendors can make proofs instantly and send them to you via email. This is a great way to check the work, make corrections and collaborate with others before deciding on the final wording.

Later, we will discuss benchers. Often, the invitation vendor can supply benchers as well. This could simplify some of your planning.

## *Content*

Much of the content of an invitation is standard with one or two stylistic choices. A typical invitation has both a Hebrew and an English side. If you cannot read the Hebrew side, then get help from someone who can proofread the final draft for accuracy.

💡 If needed, the vendor should be sensitive to and knowledgeable of invitation wording in the event of unusual family situations such as divorced parents. A vendor with experience can suggest appropriate wording.

⚠ Be careful choosing a font. Very ornate fonts may be beautiful but they may also be hard to read. In some cases, the postal service may not be able to decipher the

---

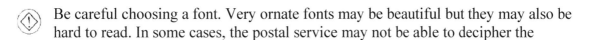
✓ See Checklist 16 – Selecting an Invitation Printer, page 103, and Checklist 18 – Invitation Content, page 105.

delivery address and the invitations won't reach their intended recipients. Even worse, you might never find out because the return address can't be read either.

> If the chosson's or kallah's last name is not the same as the parents', be sure that their full name appears somewhere on the invitation. Otherwise, a friend of the chosson or kallah may get the invitation and not realize who is getting married. Also, guests may write gift checks using the wrong last name.

If you have guests who are not familiar with Jewish sensitivities related to dress, you might want to add a line to the invitation such as:

*Modest Attire Requested*

Hopefully, those who do not understand exactly what you mean will call to find out. More detailed information about proper etiquette could be placed in a wedding program described below in section I.5.4, p. 78.

> Consider the following sticky situation: Guests are invited to a Jewish wedding who are very unaware of proper etiquette. This may lead to considerable embarrassment to the host, to these guests and possibly to others. To make matters worse, the host feels uneasy about approaching the guests directly for fear of causing even more ill will. If you are involved in such a situation, I may have an answer for you – include a note in the invitation directing the guests to the following Web site:

jewishweddings.home.mindspring.com/etiquette.html

It is a simple, direct list of basic proper behavior for Jewish weddings. The best part is that since you didn't write it, you are not implicating any particular guest in any particular behavior.

## **Invitation Information**

Your vendor will need specific information before completing your order. You can select the style and other options earlier, but the final printing must wait until all information is obtained. Be prepared to collect the following:
- Names – Hebrew and English
    - Chosson
    - Kallah
    - Chosson's parents
    - Kallah's parents
    - Grandparents (optional)
- Wedding date
- Kabbalas panim time
- Chuppah time
- Hall name and address
- Return addresses (typically parents of chosson and kallah)

## Logo

You may want a logo representing the initials of the couple to place on the front of the invitation. See Figure 2. This logo may also be used on the benchers. Invitation vendors may be able to accept a paper copy of a logo design, but many prefer a soft copy in some specific computer graphics format.

Figure 2 - Sample Logo

If you are not skilled in the art of computer graphics and you don't know of someone who is, the invitation vendor may be able to recommend someone.

## Response Cards

Response cards are short and simple. You may want to ask prospective guests if they prefer a certain type of meal (if you are offering a choice). Also, you may want to ask the guests if they can only attend the chuppah. That will save you the cost of a meal for someone who wants to come but cannot stay for the entire wedding.

It is prudent to place a number on the back of each response card. This number should match the invitation number in your guest list. It will provide identity in the event someone sends a response card back without a name. Alternatively, you can place this number on the return card envelope in case someone returns the envelope and forgets to include the card.

The response cards should include a respond-by date which, as mentioned above, should be about four weeks before the wedding date.

### Alternate Response Options

You might be tempted to try an alternative method of obtaining responses. For example:

- Ask guests to email or call in a response
- Use a Web-based invitation service

My experience with email or call-back responses is that they don't work. People simply will not get around to it and you will be stuck calling most of your guests. Web-based invitation services are new. I am not sure how effective they are for weddings.

## Directions

Driving directions included in the invitation are helpful for out-of-town guests. The hall may be able to provide direction cards. Even though many people have GPS systems or use on-line direction services, others still rely on these cards. Be sure that they include the full street address and phone number for the hall that can be used on the wedding day.

## Mailing

Addressing hundreds of envelopes is a very big chore. If you are computer savvy, you can print envelopes or labels from your computer using your list of guests from a spreadsheet. I recommend labels over printing directly on the envelopes for the following reasons.

- Printers generally don't feed envelopes well. Several will be ruined and the printer may be damaged as well.
- Mistaken labels can simply be reprinted without ruining the envelopes. Even after they are affixed to the envelopes, they can often be removed and replaced with correct ones.

Clear labels look better than plain white ones. Colored labels may look nice if you can get them to match the envelopes. If you will be addressing the envelopes by hand, then print out a guest list for reference.

It is very important to keep the envelopes in alphabetical order as you may have to refer to them several times prior to mailing. For example, you may need to check or update an address. If the envelopes are not in order, then each time you want to find one, you will have to look through all of them.

## Postage

Be sure to affix the proper postage to your invitations. After including the invitation, response card, response card envelope (with return postage) and directions card, the package could easily exceed the one-ounce limit for standard postage. U.S. postal rates for regular envelopes require a standard rate stamp for the first ounce and a specific, additional rate stamp for each additional ounce. Note that square envelopes require an additional charge. To remove all doubt, take them to your nearest post office for proper handling.

A simple touch would be to use wedding-theme stamps available from your local post office. They are the same price as regular postage and enhance the appearance of the invitations.

Remember that invitations addressed to foreign countries require additional postage. You can calculate postage by visiting the U.S. Postal Service Web site at *www.usps.com* (yes *com*, not *gov*).

United States postage is of no use on a response card returned from a foreign country. To provide return postage, purchase International Reply Coupons at your nearest post office. See Figure 3. Your foreign guests can redeem these coupons in any member country of the Universal Postage Union (which includes most countries). See Web site [2], p. 140 for a list of member countries.

*Part I – Wedding Planning Concepts*

Figure 3 – International Response Coupon

## *Advance Notice*

Don't wait for the invitation to inform close family and friends about the wedding date. Tell them directly as soon as possible to minimize scheduling conflicts.

## *Benchers*

Many families have benchers printed to commemorate the wedding. Typical prices range from about 50¢ to $5 each, depending on size and style. Some are as simple as a single laminated page, whereas others may contain numerous songs and prayers.

💡 Be sure that the benchers contain sheva brachos and the introduction to sheva brachos – not all of them do. If you produced a logo for the invitations, be sure you use it on the benchers as well.

💡 Don't rely on finding clean benchers after the wedding to save as souvenirs. Distribute benchers to close family members before the wedding for keepsakes. Since people leave the wedding at various times, you don't need one bencher per person seated at the meal. In addition to those that you want to save, order about half as many benchers as guests.

💲 Some larger cities have a gemach for benchers. Some shuls have benchers available to borrow as well.

# I.3.3 Accommodations✓

Hopefully, most of your guests will be self-sufficient. But likely, some will need assistance with travel and/or housing arrangements. You have already helped your guests by including directions with the invitations. This section describes other types of arrangements that you may have to make.

---

✓ See Checklist 21 – Accommodations, page 108; Checklist 22 – Chartering a Bus, page 109; and Checklist 23 – Bus Passengers, page 110.

*The Orthodox Jewish Wedding Planner*

## General Hotel Information

Out-of-town guests may need hotel information. Some halls can arrange discount accommodations, and many hotels will negotiate group rates for weddings. If you make such arrangements, pass the details on to your out-of-town guests.

## Other Housing Arrangements

If you are housing guests with neighbors or friends, be sure you keep straight who goes where, and when.

## Buses

If you have a number of guests traveling from one city to another for the wedding, consider renting a charter bus. I have taken such bus trips several times and found them quite enjoyable. However, organizing this is a significant chore. If possible, find a good friend who would want to ride the bus to also organize it. Give that person this section to read. First decide who will pay. Some families provide this service to their guests free of charge, but it is certainly reasonable to ask for guests to pay for their own ride since the cost is usually much less than individual driving expenses and the ride is much less stressful.

When organizing a charter bus, keep several things in mind:
- Determine the interest level by asking guests if they would want to take a bus. Count only definite answers. Let the guests know that the bus will only be available if there is sufficient interest.
- Compute the charge for each guest based on an estimate of how many are coming. Be sure to include a tip for the driver in the computation.
- Returning any surplus funds to the guests, or collecting any shortfall from them, is awkward. Plan to fill any small funding gap yourself, and use any surplus funds for snacks and drinks for the guests during the ride.
- Departure and return times must be firmly set. Guests must know exactly when to arrive and when they must be back on the bus to return. Buses from weddings usually leave early, and if the wedding is delayed, they may even leave before the meal.
- Someone on the bus must be responsible for checking the guest list to be sure everyone has boarded. Give this person the bus passenger checklist, which should include cell phone numbers of each passenger. See Checklist 23, p. 118.

## I.3.4 Honorees✓

Several honors are conferred at a Jewish wedding. Distributing these honors is a wedding-planning activity requiring a great deal of cooperation between the two families. The exact list of honors may vary depending on customs, but fortunately there are many to give out. Hopefully, a consensus will be easy to achieve. The following is a description of typical honors.

---

✓ See Checklist 24 – Participants, page 111.

*Part I – Wedding Planning Concepts*

## Mesader Kiddushin

This was described in section I.1.2. Here I simply reiterate that it is the first and most important honor. Be sure to review your wedding plans with the mesader kiddushin. The issues that could arise are numerous.

## Arev Kablan

An arev kablan is one who acts as a guarantor for another. Not all rabbis require this, but if they do, each family will need to appoint someone to fill this role. Ask your rabbi for details.

## Witnesses

Several facets of the wedding ceremony require pairs of witnesses. By Jewish law, each pair must consist of two Orthodox Jewish men who are not closely related (ideally, not at all related) to either the chosson or the kallah or to each other.

### Document Witnesses

Some witnesses must sign their Hebrew name on wedding documents. These witnesses are:
- Eidei tenaim – Witnesses who sign the conditional agreements
- Eidei kethuba – Witnesses who sign the wedding document

Make sure that they know how to spell their Hebrew names correctly. There are various customs as to whether or not surnames are included in the signatures. These would also have to be written in Hebrew.

### Other Witnesses

- Eidei kiddushin – Witnesses to the marriage ceremony
- Eidei yichud – Witnesses who stand outside the yichud room after the chuppah ceremony

Some follow the custom that the eidei kiddushin and eidei yichud are the same people.

## Reading the Marriage Documents

Generally, two documents are read during the wedding. The tenaim, written in Hebrew, is read at the chosson's tisch, just prior to when the mothers break the plate. The kethuba, written in Aramaic, is read under the chuppah. Needless to say, those who read these documents must be sufficiently skilled in reading those languages.

## Holding the Chuppah

If you have a chuppah that requires individuals to hold the poles, remember to designate these people. They might have to stand longer than anyone else, so they should be fit to do so.

*The Orthodox Jewish Wedding Planner*

## The Blessings

Seven blessings are recited under the chuppah. These are the first set of sheva brachos. There is another set after the meal. Some of the blessings are shorter and easier to read, while others are more involved. Consider this as you decide whom to honor with each blessing.

> Give these honorees advance notice in case they need time to practice. Also, let them know that they should not drink from the cup after their bracha.

The application of various customs will determine how many people are needed to recite these blessings. In some customs, a different person says each one. In others, some or most of them are said by one person.

## Chazzans

Several songs are customarily sung under the chuppah. These may be sung by a member of the orchestra or the chazzan of a shul. You may also consider a friend or relative – or even groups of friends or relatives. Typically, the three songs that are sung under the chuppah are:

- *Mi Adir* — When the chosson arrives under the chuppah
- *Mi Bon Siach* — When the kallah arrives under the chuppah and proceeds to circle the chosson seven times
- *Im Eshkachech* — After the last blessing, prior to breaking the glass

> There are many beautiful tunes for these songs. Whoever sings them should use a melody that he is familiar with and can sing well. A simple tune sung well is much nicer than a difficult tune sung poorly. See section III.2, p. 130, for the text of these songs.

See section I.1.4, p. 23, and Checklist 6, p. 92, for variations on what is sung.

## Benching

After the meal, the guests that are still around recite the benching and sheva brachos. One person is selected to lead the benching. He should be someone with experience since the beginning of the benching is different than at other meals. See Blessings 11, p. 133.

At the end of the meal, the same seven blessings said under the chuppah are repeated but in a slightly different order. The person leading the benching says the last one (which was the first one under the chuppah). The blessings in the benchers should reflect the order for after the meal. Select six additional men to say the other six blessings. See Blessings 10, p. 132.

## Backups

You should plan for backup honorees in case the originals unexpectedly don't show up. Also, if necessary, one person may be given multiple honors.

*Part I – Wedding Planning Concepts*

# I.4 Help✓

Several people can help your guests during the actual wedding to make it more a time for you to enjoy your family and friends and less a time for tracking details.

## *Wedding Coordinator*

A wedding coordinator can be instrumental in making the wedding run smoothly and may relieve a lot of stress. Often the coordinator is a woman who makes sure that the kallah is in the right place at the right time. She also organizes the processional down the aisle, and coordinates the important wedding transitions, such as ushering the mothers to break the plate and coordinating when the chosson meets the kallah for the badeken.

## *Ushers*

Ushers also can be very helpful. Having just two additional people at a wedding can make a big difference. Some things ushers can do are:
- Place the wedding programs on the seats by the chuppah
- Place "Reserved" signs on the first row or two of seats for family members
- Direct the men and women to the proper sides of the chuppah aisle. The men should sit on the side that the chosson will be standing. If the chosson and kallah face the guests, the chosson will be standing on the right side of the chuppah as viewed by the guests, and the men should sit on the right side of the aisle. If the chosson and kallah face away from the guests, the men should sit on the left side of the aisle.
- Discourage people from walking on the runner
- Help people be seated who need assistance
- Provide runner service to send messages between people and to bring things from one side of the hall to the other
- Hand out favors, etc.
- Help with seating at the meal

Given the amount of human interaction involved in these activities, it would be wise to select people with above average social skills.

## *Babysitters*

If you plan to invite lots of children, you may also want to have people available to help watch them. Be sure to delineate responsibilities carefully so that you do not overwhelm the babysitters with too many children.

## *Announcer*

Under the chuppah, someone announces who gets each honor. This person can provide more general assistance as well. For instance, he should:
- Learn the correct pronunciation of names and titles
- Make sure the wine and wineglass are properly placed near the chuppah
- Make sure a siddur and cards for the sheva brachos are prepared (or this guide)

---

✓ See Checklist 24 – Participants, page 111, and Checklist 25 – Announcer Responsibilities, page 114.

*The Orthodox Jewish Wedding Planner*

- Make sure the kittel and tallis are in place
- Make sure a small table is placed near the chuppah for the items mentioned above
- Verify that the honorees and their backups are present
- Remind guests to turn off cell phones and refrain from talking during the ceremony
- Be prepared to take the candles from the parents after they arrive under the chuppah
- Be sure the kallah circles the chosson in the proper direction – counterclockwise
- Keep count to be sure the kallah circles the chosson seven times
- Position the microphone so that the guests can hear the proceedings
- Take responsibility for the kethuba after it is given to the kallah
- Collect the kittel and whatever else may be left under the chuppah after the ceremony

Whoa, this is a lot! Perhaps the helper needs some help. In any case, for all of the above things to get done, someone has to do them.

# I.5 Detailed Planning

## I.5.1 Dressing Up✓

Women are particular about what they wear. If you are a woman reading this, you already know that. If you are a man, be prepared. Every mother, grandmother, sister and niece is going to want to dress to-the-hilt for the wedding.

### *The Wedding Dress*

Let's start from the top. The wedding dress is clearly the most elaborate garment at the wedding; at least it should be. If you have deep pockets you could easily spend thousands. But there are options.

Again, gemachs can save you lots of money. A well-stocked gemach will have a wide array of very beautiful dresses which do not compromise on quality or style. Prepare for several expenses when borrowing a wedding dress from a gemach. In addition to a small rental fee, it must be professionally cleaned and sometimes altered to fit properly. In total, using a gemach dress may cost a few hundred dollars.

A mid-range option is to employ a seamstress to make a custom dress. Be sure to use a reliable seamstress with a good client record. You may be able to have a beautiful custom dress made for less than the price of a commercial dress rental. Think vendor basics (section I.2, p. 32) when selecting a seamstress – especially availability. You will want the dress completed well before the wedding.

Buying or renting a gown from a wedding boutique or large wedding supplier can be difficult. Prevailing gown styles often stray significantly from Jewish standards of modesty. If you are getting a gown from this source, be prepared for significant alterations.

### Sheitel

There are many customs regarding when a kallah begins to cover her hair. See section I.1.4, p. 23. If the kallah will need a sheitel at the wedding, remember to prepare it beforehand.

### Think Comfort

Jewish weddings are lively and include a lot of activity on the part of the kallah. This creates a major wardrobe challenge. The clothing must not only be beautiful, but practical and comfortable. For instance, a long wedding train may be elegant but would be a disaster during the wedding dances. Unless you plan to designate someone to carry it around for the entire wedding, consider a smaller or removable train. Alternatively, some wedding dresses provide a bustle designed to pin up the train to prevent it from dragging.

---

✓ See Checklist 19 – Wardrobe, page 106.

Also, be sure the wedding dress is not too hot. This applies in the winter as well as the summer since most halls are about the same temperature all year long.

Think about shoes. Some women wear one pair of flat comfortable shoes during the entire wedding, knowing that no one can see them anyway. If the kallah wants to wear fancier shoes during the ceremony, then she should certainly have a more comfortable pair for dancing.

## Gowns

What applies to the wedding dress will also apply to the other gowns.

If you want several girls to wear the exact same color, the price will increase significantly. In this case, the dresses will almost certainly need to be custom made. Also, you will have to purchase a large amount of fabric in a single lot to assure a perfect match. If any one young lady backs out for any reason, everyone else will feel slighted, causing a lot of ill will.

It would be better to specify compatible colors such as autumn or pastel to give each person a wider choice. Again, larger cities have gemachs for these gowns as well.

## Related Preparation

Women typically pay a lot of attention to their makeup, hair and nails before the wedding. The arrangements you will need to make depend on your preferences. They can be as simple as buying special supplies to do it yourself, as convenient as stopping by a salon on the way to the wedding, or as personal as hiring professionals to come to the wedding hall. However you decide, be sure you give yourself enough time to get the job done.

 Don't get me started on up-dos!

## Changing Clothes

Women often have their hair and makeup done in one set of clothing and later change into their formal wedding dresses and gowns. Therefore, it is imperative that they be able to get out of the first set of clothing and into the second set without pulling anything over their heads. Changing into or out of anything without buttons or zippers could ruin their preparations.

## For the Men

Men are easier to dress than women, but you still must consider what they will wear as well.

### Tuxedos

If you are renting tuxedos, ask your rabbi if they must be checked for shatnes.

Every member of the wedding party who is to get a tuxedo will have to be fitted. If people are coming from out of town, then use a nationwide service that can measure them near where they live, at their convenience. After you pick up the tuxedos, have each person try on his own as soon as possible. Sizing mistakes occur frequently.

## Special Clothes

In certain circumstances, you may want the men in the wedding party to be dressed according to local custom. This can be anything from kilts in Scotland to top hats in London to streimels in Boro Park. Do not take anything for granted if you have special requirements.

## In Any Case

A wedding is a special occasion, so even if you will be wearing standard fine clothing, this is a good opportunity to get that new hat, suit or pair of shoes that you have been putting off.

## For the Chosson

In addition to the items mentioned above, the chosson has some special considerations for the chuppah ceremony, depending on family customs. Wearing a kittel is very common. You can purchase one at your local Jewish bookstore. In some families, the chosson wears an overcoat over the kittel. In yet other communities, a tallis is draped over the chosson and kallah. Check with your rabbi for the community and family customs applicable to your wedding.

## I.5.2 Wedding Activities

Jewish weddings have a set structure and are very predictable. This is good as it makes your planning easier.

### *Kabbalas Panim*

The kabbalas panim starts as two events. The kallah greets guests in one room while the chosson greets guests in another.

The kallah walks in soon after the kabbalas panim starts, escorted by her mother and mother-in-law-to-be, often accompanied by a musical fanfare.

The chosson, the fathers and then mesader kiddushin are together at the chosson's tisch. The mesader kiddushin will direct the signing of the tenaim and the kethuba as well as other activities per applicable laws and customs.

The chosson may choose to give a short speech in which he concludes the study of a tractate of the Talmud. At Chabad weddings, the chosson recites a traditional piece entitled *Ma'amar Lecha Dodi*.

Eventually, the tenaim are read followed by the mothers breaking a plate.

## Badeken

Soon after the kabbalas panim, the chosson is escorted by the fathers and many of the male guests to meet the kallah and put on her veil. After he does so, the fathers each bless the bride.

Note that the badeken is only for the first marriage of a woman. There is no badeken at the wedding of a previously married woman.

The badeken ceremony is traditionally very joyous, with the chosson being accompanied by a large crowd and lively music. According to Chabad customs, however, this is a more serious and somber ceremony; the chosson approaches the kallah with intense concentration to the music of *"The Alter Rebbe's Niggun of Four Stanzas."* You can hear this tune at Web site [6], p. 140. Members of the Chofetz Chaim community also escort the chosson to the kallah at the badeken with a more serious melody.

☺ The badeken is one of the most beautiful and emotional events of the wedding celebration. Photographs of this moment can keep the memory fresh for years. However, mothers who want to set the veil straight after the chosson places it on the kallah are a common obstacle for photographers. This can greatly interfere with capturing a very fleeting moment. Better would be for the mothers to wait until after the chosson leaves, at which point they will have ample time to straighten the veil to any desired level of perfection.

## Procession

Somehow the chosson and kallah have to get from the back of the chuppah room to the chuppah. Always, the chosson precedes the kallah. Other than that, any variations have little Jewish legal significance. In many weddings only the chosson and his parents walk down the aisle, followed by the kallah and her parents. Other weddings stage a full parade. As you add more members to the spectacle consider the following order.

- Groomsmen
- Chosson's siblings
- Chosson's other relatives
- Chosson's grandparents
- Chosson with his parents
- Bridesmaids
- Kallah's siblings
- Kallah's other relatives
- Kallah's grandparents
- Flower girl / ring bearer
- Kallah with her parents

Alternatively, if the entourage is not too large, have the chosson enter first, the relatives next, and the kallah last. Note that Chabad weddings specifically have very limited processions.

⚖️ If you are including a flower girl and ring bearer, note that the younger they are the cuter the effect but the greater the risk that they don't make it down the aisle. Make sure help is close at hand. Also, the ring bearer should *not* carry the actual ring. Use a toy ring secured to a pillow by a small thread.

Typically, the chosson and kallah are escorted to the chuppah by their respective parents. The German custom used to be to have the fathers escort the chosson and the mothers escort the kallah. This is still the Chabad custom.

Some families have the custom that the parents escort the kallah only partially toward the chuppah and then the chosson goes out to meet the kallah and bring her under the chuppah.

The procession can be a source of stress for couples with divorced parents. Divorced grandparents can easily walk down separately or not at all, with little impact. Divorced parents, on the other hand, can make procession-planning very dicey. In most cases, there is no ideal solution; the best one can expect to achieve is the least bad solution. If it is any consolation, those in this situation should know that they are not alone. Unfortunately, this is a common occurrence. If neither parent is remarried and there is minimal animosity between them, then they may walk their child down together. It can be awkward but I have seen it done more than once. Space here does not permit investigation of all possibilities so, in general, get advice from your rabbi and come up with a plan early.

*The Orthodox Jewish Wedding Planner*

## Positions

Lots of people crowd around the chuppah during the wedding ceremony. A little organization will help keep things running smoothly. Figure 4 shows a typical setup. The announcer (F) should be aware of the general plan to help people find their places.

**Figure 4 – Chuppa Ceremony Positions**

*The following list identifies those in the figure.*

- A. Kallah
- B. Chosson
- C. Mothers
- D. Fathers
- E. Mesader kiddushin
- F. Announcer
- G. Chazzan
- H. Honoree (approaching for an honor)
- I. Honorees (after their honors)
- J. Table for wine

Person H is any one of those participating under the chuppah, such as the one who reads the kethuba, the eidei kiddushin, and those who recite one of the sheva brachos. After their participation, they stand by the chuppah as shown by people I. The honorees who recite the brachos should do so standing under the chuppah and facing the chosson and kallah.

*Part I – Wedding Planning Concepts*

## Circling the Chosson

After the kallah reaches the chuppah, she circles the chosson counterclockwise escorted by the mothers. The mother of the chosson should be on the inside, to the left of the kallah, while the mother of the kallah should be toward the outside, to the right of the kallah. If the kallah has a dress with a long train, then one of the mothers should hold it so as not to have it wrap around the legs of the chosson.

Photo 11 – Tripping-Hazard Train

## The Chuppah Ceremony

The mesader kiddushin will guide the chuppah ceremony. Basically, the next step is that the mesader kiddushin will recite the blessings for nesuin and have the chosson and kallah drink from the cup of wine. The text of the various blessings can be found in section III.2 – Chuppah, p. 130.

## The Wedding Ring

The mesader kiddushin will ask the chosson if the ring is solely his. He will ask the witnesses to inspect the ring to determine if it is a sheva p'ruta (is worth a minimal financial value). The chosson will hold the ring in his right hand and say (usually with the help of the mesader kiddushin):

*Harey at m'kudeshes li b'taba'as zu, k'das Moshe v'Yisrael.*

which means "Behold, you are betrothed to me with this ring according to the law of Moses and Israel." The chosson then places the ring on the right index finger of the kallah. The ring does not have to pass the middle joint.

The rest of the ceremony is listed in section I.5.5 – Wedding Day Schedule, p. 83.

## The Reception

The main purpose of guests at the wedding is to bring joy to the chosson and kallah. And the main vehicle for this mitzvah is through dancing. The dancing starts in earnest immediately after the chuppah ceremony and continues throughout the reception.

To increase the enjoyment for the chosson and kallah, the dancing is enhanced with various gimmicks such as costumes, toys, signs, hats, etc. Most of these items are brought by friends and relatives but you may want to add some yourself.

One good source for unusual and inexpensive fun items is the Oriental Trading Company. You can find it on the Internet at Web site [3], p. 140. Plan to use the stuff you buy there only once and you will not be disappointed by their meager quality. Shop around. There are other sites as well. Remember that many items have small parts and caution should be used around very small children. It would be wise to place someone in charge of the shtick so that they are used as intended.

I would not recommend putting an inordinate amount of time, money or effort into shtick. The chosson and kallah will be very busy giving their attention to all of their guests and might not be able to show as much appreciation to a very elaborate shtick as they would like.

## Favors

You may want to give souvenirs to your guests to help them remember the occasion. Typically, the benchers serve this purpose, but if you want something else there are several options such as imprinted kippoth or custom candy bars. Kippoth are a good idea if your guests may not bring their own.

A word of caution: some guests may be tempted to take extra favors to give as gifts to their family and friends. This may result in other guests not getting their own. Consider an orderly distribution of favors such as placing one at each seat or appointing someone to distribute them.

## Arches

Often, the kallah (and sometimes the chosson with her) enters the reception through a set of arches. These may be available from a local gemach. Alternatively, they can be made from anything that won't cause too much damage as the kallah runs through. For instance, you can use ribbons suspended with helium-filled balloons. Without special props, the women guests can simply clasp hands in pairs to form a row of arches.

Photo 12 – Through the Arches

## Parasol

For some reason, unbeknownst to me, the kallah often dances with a parasol for a short time. Again, this may be available at a gemach, or some clever person may be able to fabricate one.

## I.5.3 Other Events✓

This section discusses several events that occur before and after the wedding day. Not all of them are mandatory.

### *L'Chayim*

Often people make an impromptu party on the evening of the engagement. Family and friends gather to celebrate the good news. Like any party, it can be simple or elaborate, but more typically it is very informal. It is usually held in the home of the chosson or kallah, or a friend or family member whose home has more space.

### *Vort*

The vort is another engagement party, similar to the l'chayim. It is intended for a larger group, so refreshments and space should be planned accordingly. It is a planned event that occurs within a couple weeks of the engagement. It is meant to share the simcha of the engagement with the wider community and with relatives from farther away.

A vort is not obligatory. If most of your relatives and friends joined in the l'chayim, you may elect to pass on this.

If parents are coming from out of town for the vort, then soon after would be a good time to meet and set the wedding plans in motion.

### *Showers*

Wedding showers are customarily made for the kallah by friends and family members. They are also not mandatory. Parents and the couple should not have to plan them, though they may provide input into whom to invite (if asked).

### *Ufruf*

On the shabbos prior to the wedding, the chosson is given an aliyah in shul. If the chosson is able, the shul may give him the last aliyah, in which case he would also say the haftorah. Soft candy that has been wrapped in bags or tulle and tied with a ribbon before Shabbos is distributed to members of the congregation. It is customary to throw the candy at the chosson when he is finished. In addition to preparing the candy, the family may wish to sponsor kiddush in the shul. The only other preparations would be to make arrangements for friends and family members from out of town who wish to attend. Note that the Sephardic custom is to not have an ufruf. See Shabbat Chatan below.

The German custom is *not* to throw candy in the shul for this or any other occasion. The ufruf in German shuls (pronounced aufruf) is more low key. Often the chosson does not get the last aliyah and the family may not sponsor a kiddush in the shul. They may invite friends over to their home after services.

---

✓ See Checklist 2 – Timing, page 80; Checklist 27 – Sheva Brachos Schedule, page 116; Checklist 28 – Sheva Brachos Guests, page 117; and Checklist 29 – Sheva Brachos Guest Suggestions, page 118.

For some Chassidim, a young man is given his first streimel during this Shabbos, which he then wears to the chuppah.

## *Shabbos Kallah*

Like the ufruf, the Shabbos Kallah is also on the Shabbos prior to the wedding. Basically, the kallah entertains her friends and other women of the community at her house. Like many other events, this one may be simple or elaborate. Women may linger until shalosh seudos, so preparations should be made accordingly.

## *Henna*

Henna is a custom of some Sephardic communities that occurs a few days before the wedding. A festive reception is held where the kallah is dressed in a very elaborate gown accompanied by family and friends.

⚠ Henna actually refers to a plant from which a dye high in tannin (tannic acid) is produced. Part of the celebration is the application of that dye to the palms of the hand. The dye causes a discoloration of the skin that may last for several weeks. A note of caution: henna dying is an Eastern cultural art. It has recently become a Western phenomenon, but be aware that some uneducated or unscrupulous vendors may sell dangerous chemicals such as paraphenylenediamine in place of, or in addition to, the authentic henna dye. These chemicals are illegal and can cause burns. See Web site [5], p. 140.

## *Chosson Mohl*

Some Chassidim, even those who have the chosson and kallah not see each other for the week prior to the wedding; will have them join family members for a meal before the wedding.

## *Sheva Brachos*

For the first seven days of marriage, the wedding blessings (sheva brachos) are said at certain meals. These meals are customarily referred to as sheva brachos because of the blessings that are said at them. At least ten Jewish men should be present, and at least one of them should not have been at the wedding or any prior sheva brachos meal. This "new person" requirement is not necessary on Shabbos.

**Photo 13 – Sheva Brachos**

The sheva brachos period may be shorter than seven days in certain cases of second marriages. Ask your rabbi. Sheva brachos are said when the proper conditions are met, but there does not seem to be a requirement to have any certain number of sheva brachos meals. However, it is typical to have one almost every evening and at least two on Shabbos.

Many sheva brachos meals are prepared by family or friends who want to share in the simcha. Accept offers graciously as this will allow you to focus on other aspects of the wedding and will also allow others to benefit from participating in the simcha. Ideally, your involvement in sheva brachos should be limited to letting people who want to help know who else is helping and to provide suggestions for invitees. Give the respective checklists to those planning the sheva brachos (Checklist 28 – Sheva Brachos Guests, p. 125).

☺ Sheva brachos take a lot of time, effort and money to prepare on the part of many people. It is imperative that the chosson and kallah make every effort to show up on time. A delay of up to half an hour may be tolerable, but more than that places a significant burden on the hosts and guests.

## *Shabbat Chatan*

As mentioned earlier, Sephardim do not generally have an ufruf on the Shabbos preceding the wedding. However, they do have a similar custom on the Shabbos following the wedding. On this day, the chosson and several relatives are called to the Torah and candy is thrown.

## I.5.4 What to Bring✓

A Jewish wedding requires several things to be in their proper places. Some are critical, and missing them could cause a significant delay. Other things are optional. Some of these items have been mentioned in other sections, but are repeated here to remind you to bring them to the hall on the wedding day. Many of these things require special preparation, so don't wait for the wedding day to round them up. Personal items such as cell phones, cameras and purses are not discussed here.

### *Critical Items*

#### Chuppah

Hopefully, the hall, caterer or florist has provided the chuppah. But if not, do not forget to bring it from wherever you get it.

#### Documents

Don't forget the paperwork. Section I.1.4 describes the preparation of the kethuba, tenaim, pre-nups and marriage license. All of these must be at the wedding. The mesader kiddushin should have a spare kethuba, tenaim and maybe even pre-nups forms.

#### Wedding Ring

Clearly, this is a critical item. It should be the property of the chosson before it is given to the kallah. It should be plain gold. According to Chabad custom, even the karat markings should be removed. You may want to have it inspected by your rabbi to ensure that it meets all necessary requirements.

Note that the kallah does not give the chosson a ring as part of the formal wedding ceremony. If the kallah wishes to give the chosson a ring, she should consult the rabbi as to how to do so in an appropriate manner.

#### Siddur or Cards with Sheva Brachos

The siddur or cards should show the brachos in large print. This guide would suffice. If some of the honorees cannot read Hebrew, then be sure that the brachos are transliterated.

#### Seating Cards and Lists

The seating cards are set up early. If you are having separate seating, place the seating cards on separate tables as well.

Bring three seating lists – one sorted by table number so that it will be easy to find extra spaces if needed; a second sorted by name so that you can find someone's seat if their card is misplaced; and a third with the list of special meal requests. Bring at least two copies of each of these lists – one for yourself and one for the caterer.

Be sure to bring the other lists as well, such as the list of honorees.

---

✓ See Checklist 26 – What to Bring, page 115.

## Plate

The plate that the mothers break should be prepared beforehand. It is hard to tell which plates might break easily and, unfortunately, few merchants will let you test them before you buy. Basically, it should be large, thin and inexpensive and should not contain markings such as "shatterproof". Wrap the plate in a cloth napkin for protection.

Breaking the plate can be a treacherous experience. If the plate does not break easily, the mothers will quickly become embarrassed and frustrated. Using excessive force to beak the plate can lead to serious injuries. Even with the correct type of plate, this can be a problem if you do not have a hard surface on which to break it. As a simple solution, I have developed the Nifty Plate Smasher. Use heavy-duty construction adhesive to glue two small bricks (5"x8") together at right angles. Paint them with spray paint and decorate them as you see fit. The result is a hard, flat surface on which plates will easily break. See Photo 14.

Photo 14 – Nifty Plate Smashers

## Benchers

Benchers are typically placed on the table before the meal. The caterer can do this for you.

## Wedding Dress

Okay, it is unlikely that you will forget this. But remember many pieces accompany the wedding dress such as a veil, tiara, train, shoes and more. So remember to bring them all.

## Chosson Clothing

As discussed in section I.1.4, the chosson may wear a kittel under the chuppah. Other customs include an overcoat for the chosson or a tallis draped over the chosson and kallah under the chuppah. Likewise, if ashes are to be placed on the forehead of the chosson as he enters the chuppah, they should also be prepared in advance.

## Chuppah Glasses and Wine

If you are bringing the wine yourself, have it checked by the mashgiach. Use white wine rather than red under the chuppah so that it will not make a serious mess if spilt.

The cup used to hold the wine for the blessings should befit the honor of the occasion. Silver would be best, but someone will have to watch it carefully so that it does not get lost.

The Chabad custom is to use a single glass goblet both for the blessings and for the chosson to step on after the chuppah ceremony.

### Glass to Step On

It's no big secret that the chosson breaks a glass at the end of the chuppah ceremony. However, some of the details are not so well known. First, like the plate, the glass should be thin and easy to break. It should not be too large so that it will be easy to step on. It would be better if it were not round so that it won't roll. Even though a goblet is most commonly used, any glass item will do.

### Wine, Cups for Sheva Brachos

Designate wine for the sheva brachos recited at the end of the meal. Don't rely on finding an extra bottle lying around. Three clean glasses are also required, which can be the stemmed glasses used at the reception. So, actually, these are not things that you need to bring. However, it is good to have them set aside early, during the meal, to avoid delays later.

### Checks

There are lots of people to pay at a wedding, so bring your checkbook. Most of the big-ticket items are paid for in advance. But you will have to pay at least some of the following service providers at the wedding.

- Hairdressers
- Makeup artists
- Photographers
- Hall
- Caterer
- Orchestra
- Florist
- Wedding coordinator
- Babysitters
- Ushers

It is also customary to give the mesader kiddushin a monetary gift, though it might be difficult to determine how much, since they often won't tell you.

## Optional Items

### Siddurim

Since the male guests will most likely daven mincha and/or maariv at some point, you may want to provide siddurim. Some people will bring their own but others may not.

### Box for Gifts

Many guests bring gifts and cards to the wedding, which may be difficult to track. The cards, especially, may have a tendency to disappear. One caterer suggested bringing a large, gift-wrapped box with a slit on top in which to deposit cards.

*Part I – Wedding Planning Concepts*

## Preparation Supplies

A common amenity is to supply the women's preparation area with a basket of supplies such as hairpins, hairspray, safety pins and hairbrushes.

## Quick-Fix Supplies

Though you cannot possibly anticipate every disaster, several items may be very useful at a wedding. Consider keeping a small box with these items nearby.
- Small sewing kit
- Bandages
- Wipes
- Motrin® and Tylenol®

One friend suggested pinning several safety pins together on the inside of your sleeve. That way, they will be handy for an emergency tear repair.

## Chuppah Mints

A few times, I have seen ushers distribute mints before the chuppah ceremony. It might reduce coughing during the ceremony, which is not typically a problem, or it might just be a nice thing to do.

## Programs

If you have guests who are not familiar with the proceedings of a Jewish wedding, you may wish to print programs. Some items to include are:
- A brief description of the course of events
- A list of procession members
- A list of the honorees
- Selected prayers
- Jewish wedding etiquette – For example, men do *not* kiss the kallah, and men and women dance separately.

Programs are placed on the seats in the chuppah room. One per every two seats is probably enough. Besides providing information, they give the guests something to read while the procession is starting. However, many things have already occurred by this time, so if you want the guests to have them sooner, place them near the seating cards.

## Candles

These are for the procession.

## Chairs for Chosson and Kallah

The comments above regarding the chuppah (p. 78) apply here as well.

## Shtick, Favors

As mentioned earlier, most of the shtick will be provided by friends. But bring whatever you also have prepared. Similarly, don't forget to bring the favors to the hall if you've taken the trouble to prepare them.

## Guest Book

I have rarely seen guest books at Jewish weddings. I don't know why not. They are inexpensive and readily available at most party stores. If you want to allow your guests to inscribe a memorable message to the new couple, this is a simple addition.

## I.5.5 Wedding Day Schedule

This section lists the events that will take place on the wedding day. It should help clarify what will happen when. Once everything is in place, things usually flow automatically. For this reason, this section does not have a corresponding checklist. You should not have to initiate each step of the wedding. The following list is also shown pictorially in Figure 5. This list is basically according to Ashkenazic customs. Differences for other customs are described in section I.1.4 – Customs, p. 23.

- Preparation
    - Caterer begins preparations
    - Women arrive at hall for makeup and hair preparation
    - Florist arrives to set up
    - Orchestra arrives to set up
    - All immediate family members arrive
    - Chosson and kallah recite individual prayers
    - Photographer photographs the chosson and kallah with their respective families

- Kabbalas Panim
    - Guests arrive
    - Chosson greets guests at the chosson's tisch
    - Kallah enters the badeken room escorted by her mother and mother-in-law to be
    - Kallah is seated and greets guests
    - Mesader kiddushin arrives
    - Mesader kiddushin instructs fathers and others to make kinyanim
    - Tenaim and kethuba documents are signed (some sign kethuba later)
    - Mothers come from the badeken room to the chosson's room
    - Tenaim document is read
    - Mothers break a plate over the back of a chair (or on Nifty Plate Smasher, p. 79)
    - Mothers return to the kallah
    - Chosson is escorted to the kallah with much fanfare
    - Chosson places the veil over the kallah
    - Fathers of the chosson and kallah bless the kallah
    - Others may also bless the kallah (e.g., grandfathers)
    - Chosson is escorted out of the badeken room
    - Mesader kiddushin places ashes on chosson's forehead

- Chuppah Ceremony
    - Guests proceed to the chuppah room to be seated. The chosson and kallah should be situated out of sight so as not to be in contact with the guests.
    - Procession starts – the critical elements are:
        - Chosson enters the chuppah with his parents
        - Chosson dons a kittel (if not done previously)

- Someone sings Mi Adir
- Kallah enters the chuppah with her parents
  - Kallah, accompanied by the mothers, circles the chosson seven times
  - Someone sings Mi Bon Siach
  - Mesader kiddushin recites the blessings of kiddushin
  - Chosson and kallah drink from the cup
  - Chosson gives the kallah the wedding ring
  - Kethuba is read
  - Chosson gives the kallah the kethuba
  - Kallah gives the kethuba to one of her relatives
  - Mesader kiddushin may say a few words
  - Sheva brachos are recited
  - Chosson and kallah drink from the cup again
  - Someone sings Im Eshkachech
  - Chosson breaks the glass
  - Chosson and kallah are escorted to the yichud room

- Reception
  - Guests proceed to the dining area and the appetizer is served
  - Family members pose for photos
  - Family (without chosson and kallah) enter the meal
  - Chosson and kallah make their grand entrance
  - Guests dance with the chosson and kallah
  - Chosson and kallah sit to eat, main course is served
  - Other activities such as speeches can occur here
  - Guests dance with the chosson and kallah a second time
  - Dessert is served
  - Benching and sheva brachos for the meal are recited
  - Cleanup

💡 At some point the men will want to recite the afternoon and/or evening prayers. People tend to start spontaneous minyanim at inopportune times and places, which could interfere with the ceremony. Plan ahead and announce the time and place for a single mincha and maariv davening.

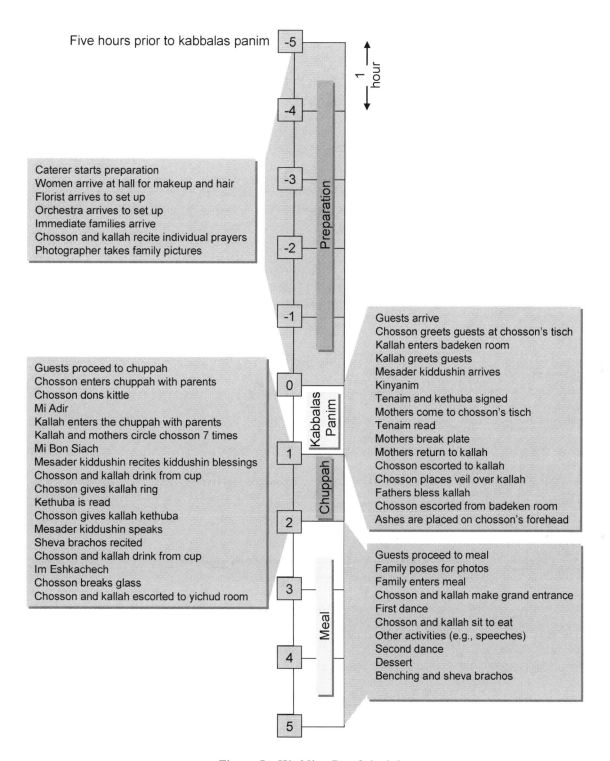

**Figure 5 – Wedding Day Schedule**

## I.5.6 After the Wedding

Wait – you're not done yet! There's more. The first chore after the wedding is cleaning up the mess. Most of this will be handled by the staff of the hall and the caterer, but you will have to take care of several items.

### Gather Up Personal Belongings

Remember to take home all of your stuff. This will include all of the changes of clothing and gifts given to the chosson and kallah. If you are taking home leftover food or flowers, you may need a lot of space. Be sure some people with extra trunk room stick around for a while to help haul everything away.

### Extra Food and Flowers

Disposing of the extra food and flowers was discussed in sections I.2.2, p. 40 and I.2.3, p. 47. If you made a plan earlier, you will be prepared now.

### Once Through

The last family member out (not the chosson or kallah) should check all areas of the hall for missing items. Make sure to get a point of contact from the hall to call in case something cannot be found. Check all of the rooms used during the wedding including dressing rooms, restrooms, etc.

### Next Stop

Now that the wedding is over, you can move on to sheva brachos as described in section I.5.3, p. 75.

# PART II – Checklists

*The Orthodox Jewish Wedding Planner –*

## II.1 Timing Checklist

This checklist includes, in chronological order, all of the major planning steps mentioned in the first part of this guide. Some items may be mentioned several times – once to prepare, once to bring, and once to set up. It is unlikely that any wedding will include all the items listed here. Cross off those items that do not apply. Once you have a date for the wedding, fill in the date column to keep yourself on track.

**Checklist 2 – Timing**

| Time Relative to Wedding | Date | Done | Task |
|---|---|---|---|
| Day of engagement | | | L'chayim |
| Within 2 weeks after engagement | | | Vort |
| ASAP | | | Choose date for wedding |
| | | | Decide wedding scope and assign costs |
| | | | Select hall |
| | | | Select caterer |
| | | | Select mesader kiddushin |
| As soon as practical | | | Select orchestra |
| | | | Select florist |
| | | | Select seamstress or other dress options |
| | | | Select hair and makeup stylists |
| 12 weeks | | | Design logo for invitations and benchers |
| 10 weeks | | | Select invitation vendor |
| | | | Select bencher vendor |
| 9 weeks | | | Decide invitation style, layout and wording |
| | | | Order invitations |
| | | | Order benchers* |
| 7 weeks | | | Receive invitations from printer |
| 6 weeks | | | Mail invitations |
| 4 weeks | | | Responses due (responses start coming in) |
| | | | Marriage license |
| | | | Assign honorees |
| | | | Arrange sheva brachos |
| | | | Rent tuxedos |
| 3 weeks | | | Finalize menu |
| 2 weeks | | | Dresses completed |
| | | | Call guests who have not responded |
| | | | Assign seats for the reception and make cards |
| | | | Coordinate music with orchestra |

*Part II – Checklists*

| Time Relative to Wedding | Date | Done | Task |
|---|---|---|---|
|  |  |  | Confirm arrangements with florist |
|  |  |  | Confirm arrangements with photographer |
| 1 week |  |  | Give caterer final count |
|  |  |  | Decide on final menu |
| 3 days |  |  | Nails |
| Shabbos before |  |  | Shabbos kallah |
|  |  |  | Ufruf |
| Day before |  |  | Pick up and try on tuxedos |
| Wedding day |  |  | Bring all necessary items |
| Week after wedding |  |  | Sheva brachos |

*Note that the bencher timing is a bit early. If you use the same vendor for benchers and invitations, you may as well order them at the same time.

## II.2 Choosing a Date Checklist

Choose a few dates. You may not be able to check all of the requirements at once. So if one date does not work out you will have a backup. Note that this, like many of the checklists, includes extra rows for items that I have not thought of that may apply in your particular case.

**Checklist 3 – Choosing a Date**

|  | Date 1 | Date 2 | Date 3 | Date 4 |
|---|---|---|---|---|
| Date |  |  |  |  |
| Time |  |  |  |  |
| Day of the week |  |  |  |  |
| Far enough in advance |  |  |  |  |
| Weather likely to be OK |  |  |  |  |
| No other family obligations |  |  |  |  |
| Key members available |  |  |  |  |
| Not on a date precluded by Jewish law |  |  |  |  |
| Near Jewish holiday |  |  |  |  |
| Near secular holiday |  |  |  |  |
| In/out of wedding season |  |  |  |  |
| Convenient time of day |  |  |  |  |
| Caterer available |  |  |  |  |
| Hall available |  |  |  |  |
|  |  |  |  |  |
|  |  |  |  |  |

## II.3 Wedding Cost Checklists

### General Scope

Simply jot down your collective decision for each of these items. A table may be a bit much, but at least you will know that you have an agreement.

**Checklist 4 – Wedding Scope**

| Item | Decision |
|---|---|
| Approximate number of guests | |
| Type of venue | |
| Mesader kiddushin | |
| General wedding location (city) | |
| | |

### Responsibility Details

Use this table to clearly delineate financial and other responsibilities. For each row, check the party that is accepting responsibility. The "Other" column is for those families fortunate enough to have a rich uncle or the like.

**Checklist 5 – Wedding Cost Details**

| | | Chosson's Parents | Kallah's Parents | Chosson | Kallah | Other |
|---|---|---|---|---|---|---|
| Hall | | | | | | |
| Caterer | | | | | | |
| Invitations | | | | | | |
| Benchers | | | | | | |
| FLOP | Flowers | | | | | |
| | Liquor | | | | | |
| | Orchestra | | | | | |
| | Photographer | | | | | |
| | Videographer | | | | | |
| Travel for the mesader kiddushin | | | | | | |
| Cost for extra guests | | | | | | |
| *Chuppah | | | | | | |
| *Mechitza | | | | | | |
| *Chosson's and kallah's chairs | | | | | | |
| Glass to break | | | | | | |
| Plate to break | | | | | | |

\* These items may depend on who can supply them (e.g., hall, caterer, and florist)

## II.4 Customs Checklist

Jewish customs vary widely. This list is just a guide. ✓ indicates a specific custom. ✗ indicates no specific custom, ~ indicates that some do and others don't. Numbers refer to notes that follow the checklist. Some items are listed even though no one has a specific custom but nonetheless it is sometimes done. Often, Jews from one community will include popular customs from other communities. Getting everyone on the same page as to which customs will prevail at your wedding will smooth out the process. The items in this list are described in section I.1.4 on page 23.

**Checklist 6 – Customs**

| Custom | Ashkenazic | Chassidic | Germanic | Sephardic | What You Plan to Do |
|---|---|---|---|---|---|
| Ufruf | ✓ | ✓ | ✓ | ✗ | |
| Streimel | ✗ | ✓ | ✗ | ✗ | |
| Shabbos kallah | ✓ | ✓ | ✗ | ✗ | |
| Henna | ✗ | ✗ | ✗ | ✓ | |
| Separating before badeken | ✗ | ✓ | 1 | ✗ | |
| Chosson mohl | ✗ | ~ | ✗ | ✗ | |
| Fasting on day of wedding | ✓ | ✓ | ✓ | ✗ | |
| Chosson to mikveh - 2 | ✓ | ✓ | ✗ | ~ | |
| Viduy in mincha | ✓ | ✓ | ✓ | ✗ | |
| Arev kablan | ✗ | ✗ | ✗ | ✗ | |
| Tenaim | ✓ | ✓ | ✗ | ✗ | |
| Prenuptial agreement | ✗ | ✗ | ✗ | ✗ | |
| Badeken | ✓ | ✓ | ✗ | ✗ | |
| Chuppah in sanctuary | ✗ | ✗ | ✓ | ✓ | |
| Chuppah outside | ✓ | ✓ | ✗ | ✗ | |
| Couple face away from the guests | 3 | ✓ | ✓ | ✗ | |
| Ashes | ✓ | ✗ | ✗ | ✗ | |
| Kittel | ✓ | ✓ | ✗ | ✗ | |
| Overcoat | ✗ | ✓ | ✗ | ✗ | |
| Thick veil | ✗ | ✓ | ✗ | ✗ | |
| Remove jewelry for chuppah | ✓ | ✓ | ✗ | ✗ | |
| Hold candles | ✓ | ✓ | 4 | ✗ | |
| Kallah circles chosson seven times | ✓ | ✓ | ✗ | ✗ | |
| Read kethuba under chuppah | ✓ | ✓ | ✓ | ✓ | |
| Mi Bon Siach | ✓ | ✓ | ✗ | 5 | |
| Tallis | ✗ | ✗ | ✓ | ✓ | |
| Chosson oath under chuppah | ✗ | ✗ | ✗ | ✓ | |
| Chosson signs kethuba | ✗ | ✗ | ✗ | ✓ | |

| Custom | Ashkenazic | Chassidic | Germanic | Sephardic | What You Plan to Do |
|---|---|---|---|---|---|
| Birchas cohanim under chuppah | ✗ | ✗ | ✗ | ✓ | |
| Psalm 128 before breaking glass | ✗ | ✗ | ✓ | ✗ | |
| Im Eshkachech before breaking glass | ✗ | ✗ | ✗ | ✗ | |
| Hair covering after yichud | ~ | ✓ | ✓ | ✗ | |
| Yichud | ✓ | ✓ | ✓ | 6 | |
| Mitzvah tanz | ✗ | 7 | ✗ | ✗ | |
| Mezinke tanz | ✓ | ✗ | ✗ | ✗ | |
| Shabbat chatan | ✗ | ✗ | ✗ | ✓ | |

Notes
1. Only for the day of the wedding.
2. Mikveh use by the chosson differs by custom. Mikveh use by the kallah is a very important halacha. See Section I.1.4, p. 23.
3. The Ashkenazic custom is for the couple to face the guests
4. The German custom is to have lit candles on a table near the chuppah.
5. There are various customs as to what Sephardim sing.
6. The chosson and kallah eat a meal together but are not sequestered in the presence of witnesses.
7. Many Chassidim do, Chabad do not.

*The Orthodox Jewish Wedding Planner –*

## II.5 Selecting a Hall Checklist

This checklist will assist you in selecting a hall. Space is provided for up to four halls. You may want to investigate more or fewer halls. Also, you do not have to fill out every item for every hall. You may be able to eliminate a hall after only a few key questions.

**Checklist 7 – Selecting a Hall**

|  | Hall 1 | Hall 2 | Hall 3 | Hall 4 |
|---|---|---|---|---|
| **Contact Information** | | | | |
| Hall name | | | | |
| Point of contact | | | | |
| Phone number | | | | |
| Email address | | | | |
| | | | | |
| **Vendor Basics** | | | | |
| Years in business | | | | |
| Jewish wedding experience | | | | |
| References | | | | |
| Availability | | | | |
| Deposit required | | | | |
| Cancellation policy | | | | |
| | | | | |
| **Location** | | | | |
| Close to home | | | | |
| Easy access | | | | |
| Ample parking | | | | |
| Safe neighborhood | | | | |
| Away from traffic congestion | | | | |
| Near lodging | | | | |
| | | | | |
| **Room for:** | | | | |
| Lobby | | | | |
| Kallah's preparation area | | | | |
| Chosson's preparation area | | | | |
| Chosson's tisch | | | | |
| Badeken | | | | |
| Chuppah | | | | |
| Yichud room | | | | |
| Family photography area | | | | |

*Part II – Checklists*

|  | Hall 1 | Hall 2 | Hall 3 | Hall 4 |
|---|---|---|---|---|
| Meal and dancing | | | | |
| Minimal changing of one area into another | | | | |
| | | | | |
| **Ambience** | | | | |
| Clean | | | | |
| Good repair | | | | |
| Well lit | | | | |
| Well decorated | | | | |
| No inappropriate decorations | | | | |
| Away from distracting noises and odors | | | | |
| Nice place for outdoor chuppah | | | | |
| Skylight for chuppah | | | | |
| Exclusive use of facility | | | | |
| | | | | |
| **Price** | | | | |
| Basic price | | | | |
| Overtime price | | | | |
| Cleaning fee | | | | |
| Chair/table/stands setup and rental fees | | | | |
| Fees for use of extra rooms | | | | |
| Liquor/soda fees | | | | |
| Coatroom service | | | | |
| Parking fees | | | | |
| | | | | |
| **Do they provide** | | | | |
| Chuppah | | | | |
| Mechitza | | | | |
| Sound system | | | | |
| Platforms | | | | |
| Chosson and kallah chairs | | | | |
| Housekeeping services | | | | |
| Emergency facility services | | | | |

*The Orthodox Jewish Wedding Planner –*

|  | Hall 1 | Hall 2 | Hall 3 | Hall 4 |
|---|---|---|---|---|
| Lodging arrangements | | | | |
| Security arrangements | | | | |
| | | | | |
| **Get signed contract from chosen hall** | | | | |

*Part II –Checklists*

# II.6 Selecting a Caterer Checklist

The same comments that apply to the hall checklist apply here as well.

**Checklist 8 – Selecting a Caterer**

|  | Caterer 1 | Caterer 2 | Caterer 3 | Caterer 4 |
|---|---|---|---|---|
| **Contact Information** | | | | |
| Business name | | | | |
| Point of contact | | | | |
| Phone number | | | | |
| Email address | | | | |
| | | | | |
| **Vendor Basics** | | | | |
| Years in business | | | | |
| Jewish wedding experience | | | | |
| References | | | | |
| Availability | | | | |
| Deposit required | | | | |
| Cancellation policy | | | | |
| | | | | |
| **Caterer Basics** | | | | |
| Reliable kosher supervision | | | | |
| Can work in a wide range of halls | | | | |
| Menu selection | | | | |
| Taste sampling | | | | |
| Sufficient staff | | | | |
| Pleasant staff | | | | |
| Enough time to eat | | | | |
| | | | | |
| **Fees** | | | | |
| Basic meal charge | | | | |
| Smorgasbord | | | | |
| Kashering fee | | | | |
| Mashgiach fee | | | | |
| Liquor fee | | | | |
| Wine service | | | | |
| Dessert service | | | | |
| Other costs | | | | |
| Cleaning fees | | | | |
| Able to negotiate rates with hall | | | | |

|  | Caterer 1 | Caterer 2 | Caterer 3 | Caterer 4 |
|---|---|---|---|---|
| **Special Requests** | | | | |
| Large challah | | | | |
| Chocolate fountain | | | | |
| Punch fountain | | | | |
| Fruit sculptures | | | | |
| Water bottles for outdoor chuppah | | | | |
| Yichud room meals | | | | |
| Crasher meals | | | | |
| Table décor | | | | |
| Wedding cake | | | | |
| | | | | |
| **Other Things** | | | | |
| Alternate dinner arrangements | | | | |
| Hall layout ideas | | | | |
| | | | | |
| **Do they provide** | | | | |
| Chuppah | | | | |
| Mechitza | | | | |
| Chosson and kallah chairs | | | | |
| Charitable distribution of leftovers | | | | |
| | | | | |
| **Get signed contract from chosen caterer** | | | | |

## II.7 Selecting a Florist Checklist

As mentioned previously, the price of flowers can vary greatly. In this table, the price of each item is given in ranges since each vendor will give you choices. For the various items, you should be able to compare the range of one florist to another. Remember to check out a flower gemach to save money.

**Checklist 9 – Selecting a Florist**

|  | Florist 1 | Florist 2 | Florist 3 | Florist 4 |
|---|---|---|---|---|
| **Contact Information** | | | | |
| Business name | | | | |
| Point of contact | | | | |
| Phone number | | | | |
| Email address | | | | |
| | | | | |
| **Vendor Basics** | | | | |
| Years in business | | | | |
| Jewish wedding experience | | | | |
| References | | | | |
| Availability | | | | |
| Deposit required | | | | |
| Cancellation policy | | | | |
| | | | | |
| **Price Ranges** | | | | |
| Bridal bouquet | | | | |
| Corsages | | | | |
| Boutonnières | | | | |
| Other bouquets | | | | |
| Decorating badeken | | | | |
| Decorating chuppah | | | | |
| Runner | | | | |
| Aisle decorations | | | | |
| Decorating the mechitza | | | | |
| Table centerpieces (women's side) | | | | |
| Table centerpieces (men's side) | | | | |
| | | | | |
| **Do they provide:** | | | | |
| Staff during wedding | | | | |
| Chuppah | | | | |
| Mechitza | | | | |
| Chosson and kallah chairs | | | | |
| Charitable disposition after | | | | |

|  | Florist 1 | Florist 2 | Florist 3 | Florist 4 |
|---|---|---|---|---|
| the wedding |  |  |  |  |
|  |  |  |  |  |
| **Get signed contract from chosen florist** |  |  |  |  |

## II.8 Selecting an Orchestra Checklist

**Checklist 10 – Selecting an Orchestra**

|  | Orchestra 1 | Orchestra 2 | Orchestra 3 | Orchestra 4 |
|---|---|---|---|---|
| **Contact Information** | | | | |
| Business name | | | | |
| Point of contact | | | | |
| Phone number | | | | |
| Email address | | | | |
| | | | | |
| **Vendor Basics** | | | | |
| Years in business | | | | |
| Jewish wedding experience | | | | |
| References | | | | |
| Availability | | | | |
| Deposit required | | | | |
| Cancellation policy | | | | |
| | | | | |
| **Orchestra Basics** | | | | |
| Know your favorite songs | | | | |
| Sound samples | | | | |
| Will cooperate with family performers | | | | |
| Play during all phases of the wedding | | | | |
| Sensitive to danger of excessive music volume | | | | |
| | | | | |
| **Price** | | | | |
| Basic price | | | | |
| Price per additional performer | | | | |
| Setup price | | | | |
| Overtime charge | | | | |
| Special instrumentation | | | | |
| Bandstand | | | | |

|  | Orchestra 1 | Orchestra 2 | Orchestra 3 | Orchestra 4 |
|---|---|---|---|---|
| Amplification equipment (including extra microphones) | | | | |
| Sound Technician | | | | |
| Other additional costs | | | | |
|  | | | | |
| **Get signed contract from chosen orchestra** | | | | |

*Part II –Checklists*

## II.9 Selecting a Photographer Checklists

This section contains several checklists: one for selecting the photographer, another for selecting the videographer (if separate from the photographer), and a third to enumerate important groupings and poses of family members that you want the photographer to take.

**Checklist 11 – Selecting a Photographer**

|  | Photo 1 | Photo 2 | Photo 3 | Photo 4 |
|---|---|---|---|---|
| **Contact Information** | | | | |
| Business name | | | | |
| Point of contact | | | | |
| Phone number | | | | |
| Email address | | | | |
| | | | | |
| **Vendor Basics** | | | | |
| Years in business | | | | |
| Jewish wedding experience | | | | |
| References | | | | |
| Availability | | | | |
| Deposit required | | | | |
| Cancellation policy | | | | |
| | | | | |
| **Photographer Basics** | | | | |
| Film or digital | | | | |
| Delivers original negatives or digital images | | | | |
| Production time | | | | |
| Number of photographers | | | | |
| Male and female photographers | | | | |
| Supplemental lighting | | | | |
| Basic cost | | | | |
| Price for extra prints | | | | |
| Image copyrights | | | | |
| | | | | |
| **Albums** | | | | |
| Number of photos in couple's album | | | | |

|  | Photo 1 | Photo 2 | Photo 3 | Photo 4 |
|---|---|---|---|---|
| Size of photos in couple's album | | | | |
| Number of photos in parents' album | | | | |
| Size of photos in parents' album | | | | |
| | | | | |
| **Photography Style** | | | | |
| How invasive will the photographer be? | | | | |
| Time devoted to posed family portraits | | | | |
| | | | | |
| Inform photographer that images may only be used with your permission | | | | |
| **Get signed contract from chosen photographer** | | | | |

## Videography

**Checklist 12 – Selecting a Videographer**

|  | Video 1 | Video 2 | Video 3 | Video 4 |
|---|---|---|---|---|
| **Contact Information** | | | | |
| Business name | | | | |
| Point of contact | | | | |
| Phone number | | | | |
| Email address | | | | |
| | | | | |
| **Vendor Basics** | | | | |
| Years in business | | | | |
| Jewish wedding experience | | | | |
| References | | | | |
| Availability | | | | |
| Deposit required | | | | |
| Cancellation policy | | | | |
| | | | | |
| **Videography Basics** | | | | |
| Basic cost | | | | |
| Associated with photographer | | | | |
| Final format (VHS, DVD, …) | | | | |
| Amount of editing included | | | | |
| Number of copies | | | | |
| Cost for extra copies | | | | |
| Final product copyrighted | | | | |
| | | | | |
| Inform videographer that images may only be used with your permission | | | | |
| **Get signed contract from chosen videographer** | | | | |

*The Orthodox Jewish Wedding Planner –*

## Poses

By identifying the critical groups of people that you want photographed, you will save time and get the photos that you want. Take as many photos as possible before the chuppah.

**Checklist 13 – Poses**

|  | Done | Before / After Chuppah | With Chosson | With Kallah | Others |
|---|---|---|---|---|---|
| 1 | | | | | |
| 2 | | | | | |
| 3 | | | | | |
| 4 | | | | | |
| 5 | | | | | |
| 6 | | | | | |
| 7 | | | | | |
| 8 | | | | | |
| 9 | | | | | |
| 10 | | | | | |
| 11 | | | | | |
| 12 | | | | | |
| 13 | | | | | |
| 14 | | | | | |
| 15 | | | | | |
| 16 | | | | | |
| 17 | | | | | |

## II.10 Guest List Sample

This table should have *one row per invitation* that you mail.

You probably do not want to use this paper copy for the guest list. A spreadsheet program such as Microsoft Excel would be much better. One advantage is that you could then sum up the Number Expected column to get an idea as to how many people you will need to feed. If you do so, be sure to include those who are coming without an invitation, such as the chosson, kallah, parents, the orchestra members and the photographers.

Add extra columns for additional information such as special meal requests.

**Column Descriptions**
- **Invitation Number** – The number placed on the back of each response card
- **Last Name** – Last name of invitee (used to sort the list)
- **Mailing Name** – Full name(s) of the invitee(s) as it will appear on the invitation envelope
- **Street Address** – Mailing street address
- **City**
- **State**
- **Zip Code**
- **Country**
- **Phone Number** – To call those who do not respond
- **Guest Category** – This identifies the guest as being invited by the kallah's side or the chosson's side. You can have as many categories as you wish, for example: "father's work," "shul," or "yeshiva friends." Choose the level of detail based on the number of invited guests.
- **Meal or Chuppah Only** – Indicates if the invitation is for the full meal or only the chuppah
- **Number Invited** – Number of guests that are included in the invitation
- **Number Expected** – Your guess as to how many of the invited people will actually attend. Even though you do not know for sure, you will probably have a pretty good idea. This can be very helpful, since the number of guests invited may be more than twice the number of those that actually come.
- **Sent** – This is a status column that you can check when you actually send the invitation. You may be collecting information and adding new invitees over a period of time. You need to track which invitations have been sent and which have not. In a spreadsheet, you can add additional status columns as needed.
- **Number Responded** – Fill this in when you get the response cards back. This gives the exact number of people to expect.
- **Answers to other questions** – If, on the response card, you asked other questions, such as food preference, then those answers go here. You will need an additional column for each question.

**Checklist 14 – Guest List Sample**

| | | | | | | | | | | |
|---|---|---|---|---|---|---|---|---|---|---|
| | | | | | | | | | | Invitation Number |
| | | | | | | | | | | Last Name |
| | | | | | | | | | | Mailing Name |
| | | | | | | | | | | Street Address |
| | | | | | | | | | | City |
| | | | | | | | | | | State |
| | | | | | | | | | | Zip Code |
| | | | | | | | | | | Country |
| | | | | | | | | | | Phone Number |
| | | | | | | | | | | Guest Category |
| | | | | | | | | | | Meal/Chuppah Only |
| | | | | | | | | | | Number Invited |
| | | | | | | | | | | Number Expected |
| | | | | | | | | | | Sent |
| | | | | | | | | | | Number Responded |
| | | | | | | | | | | Answers to other questions |

## II.11 Seating List Sample

Just like the guest list above, this list is best implemented in a spreadsheet program. A major advantage is that you would then be able to easily create three printouts – one sorted by name, another sorted by table number and yet another with all of the special meal requests.

There should be *one row per seating card*.

**Column Descriptions**
- **Guest Name** – The name as it will appear on the seating card
- **Last Name** – Used to sort the seating assignments by name
- **Number of Seats** – How many people are seated with this card
- **Table Number** – Assigned table where the guest(s) will sit. This can be used to sort the guests by table number
- **Special Meal** – Used to track special meal requests

**Checklist 15 – Seating List Sample**

| Guest Name | Last Name | Number of Seats | Table Number | Special Meal |
|---|---|---|---|---|
| | | | | |

## II.12 Invitations and Benchers Checklists

This section has two checklists. The first addresses selecting an invitation vendor, and the second tracks the information printed in the invitation.

### *Selecting a Vendor*

Note that a cancellation policy may not be relevant. Once a printing order is placed, it may be difficult to cancel.

**Checklist 16 – Selecting an Invitation Printer**

|  | Vendor 1 | Vendor 2 | Vendor 3 | Vendor 4 |
|---|---|---|---|---|
| **Contact Information** | | | | |
| Business name | | | | |
| Point of contact | | | | |
| Phone number | | | | |
| Email address | | | | |
| | | | | |
| **Vendor Basics** | | | | |
| Years in business | | | | |
| Jewish wedding experience | | | | |
| References | | | | |
| Availability | | | | |
| Deposit required | | | | |
| Cancellation policy | | | | |
| | | | | |
| **Printing Basics** | | | | |
| Virtual proofs | | | | |
| Benchers | | | | |
| Time to print invitations | | | | |
| | | | | |
| **Get signed contract from chosen printer** | | | | |

*The Orthodox Jewish Wedding Planner –*

## Invitation Information

The following information is needed to go to press. Items such as Parents' English names should be specified exactly as you would like them to appear in the invitation.

**Checklist 17 – Invitation Information**

| Item | Value |
|---|---|
| **Chosson** | |
| Hebrew name | |
| English name | |
| Parents' Hebrew names | |
| Parents' English names | |
| Grandparents' names | |
| | |
| Parents' address | |
| | |
| | |
| **Kallah** | |
| Hebrew name | |
| English name | |
| Parents' Hebrew names | |
| Parents' English names | |
| Grandparents' names | |
| | |
| Parents' address | |
| | |
| | |
| **Wedding Information** | |
| English date | |
| Hebrew date | |
| Time – kabbalas panim | |
| Time – chuppah | |
| Hall name | |
| Hall address | |
| | |

## Invitation Content

This list describes the content and preparation of the invitations. Check each item as completed.

**Checklist 18 – Invitation Content**

| Done | Item |
|---|---|
| **Invitation** | |
| | Choose a legible font |
| | Choose wording |
| | Wording includes date and time |
| | Wording includes hall name and address |
| | Chosson's and kallah's last names appear in the invitation |
| | Include request for modest attire |
| | Supply logo |
| | Use wedding-theme stamps |
| | Proper postage (including foreign postage) |
| | |
| **Direction Cards** | |
| | Determine who will provide travel direction cards |
| | Include hall's name, full street address and phone number |
| | |
| **Response Cards** | |
| | Set response date four weeks before the wedding |
| | Include special meal request selection |
| | Ask if guests will only be attending the chuppah |
| | Place invitation number on back |
| | Proper postage (including foreign postage) |
| | |
| **Benchers** | |
| | Includes sheva brachos |
| | Keep several at home for posterity |
| | |

## II.13 Wardrobe Checklist

This checklist tracks everything you will need to dress the wedding party. The details will depend on how you get each item. Check off each item as you get it.

**Checklist 19 – Wardrobe**

| Done | Item |
|---|---|
| **Kallah** | |
| | Dress (with small or removable train, crinoline, etc.) |
| | Veil |
| | Tiara |
| | Shoes (ceremony and dancing), hose |
| | Preparation clothes that don't pull over the head |
| | Sheitel |
| | Arrange for nails, hair, makeup |
| | |
| **Mothers, Sisters (one column per person)** | |
| | Dress |
| | Shoes, hose |
| | Sheitel |
| | Preparation clothes that don't pull over the head |
| | Arrange for nails, hair, makeup |
| | |
| **Chosson** | |
| | Suit |
| | Hat |
| | Tie |
| | Shoes, socks |
| | Kittel |
| | Coat |
| | Tuxedo |
| | Tallis |
| | Belt, cuff links |
| | |
| **Fathers, Brothers (one column per person)** | |
| | Suit |
| | Hat |
| | Tie |
| | Shoes, socks |
| | Tuxedo |
| | Shirt |
| | Belt, cuff links |
| | |

## II.14 Paperwork Checklist

Be sure all of the documents are in order well before the wedding. For instance there may be many requirements for a marriage license that may take time to meet. See section I.1.5I.1.4, p. 29. This list is not long but it is important. Check off each item as it is completed. These items will show up again in Checklist 26 – What to Bring.

**Checklist 20 – Documentation**

| Complete | Document |
|---|---|
|  | Kethuba |
|  | Tenaim |
|  | Prenuptial agreements |
|  | Marriage license / certificate |

## II.15 Accommodations Checklists

### Lodging/Transportation Requirements

Use this list to track those who need travel and/or lodging assistance.

**Checklist 21 – Accommodations**

| Guest | Phone | Lodging | | Transportation | |
|---|---|---|---|---|---|
| | | Needs | Arrangements | Needs | Arrangements |
| | | | | | |
| | | | | | |
| | | | | | |
| | | | | | |
| | | | | | |
| | | | | | |
| | | | | | |
| | | | | | |
| | | | | | |
| | | | | | |
| | | | | | |
| | | | | | |
| | | | | | |
| | | | | | |
| | | | | | |
| | | | | | |
| | | | | | |
| | | | | | |
| | | | | | |
| | | | | | |

## Charter Bus Planning Sheet

Two things are needed to arrange a charter bus to a wedding. The first is basic information about the trip and the second is the passenger list. I did not include a vendor selection checklist for the bus company. Hopefully, this is more of a standard service that can be chosen without too much effort.

**Checklist 22 – Chartering a Bus**

| Charter Bus Company | |
|---|---|
| Company name | |
| Point of contact | |
| Phone number | |
| Suggested driver tip | |
| Total cost | |
| Total available seats | |
| | |
| **Trip Details** | |
| Designated coordinator | |
| Boarding location | |
| Boarding time | |
| Arrival time at wedding | |
| Leave time from wedding | |
| Return time to origin | |
| | |
| **General Guest Information** | |
| Approximate number of guests | |
| Price per guest | |
| | |

## Charter Bus Passenger List

Check the attendance columns to ensure that everyone is on board coming, going and after any intermediate stops.

**Checklist 23 – Bus Passengers**

| Guest Name | Seats | Phone | Cell Phone | Paid | Attendance | | |
|---|---|---|---|---|---|---|---|
| | | | | | | | |
| | | | | | | | |
| | | | | | | | |
| | | | | | | | |
| | | | | | | | |
| | | | | | | | |
| | | | | | | | |
| | | | | | | | |
| | | | | | | | |
| | | | | | | | |
| | | | | | | | |
| | | | | | | | |
| | | | | | | | |
| | | | | | | | |
| | | | | | | | |
| | | | | | | | |
| | | | | | | | |
| | | | | | | | |
| | | | | | | | |
| | | | | | | | |
| | | | | | | | |
| | | | | | | | |
| | | | | | | | |
| | | | | | | | |
| | | | | | | | |
| | | | | | | | |
| | | | | | | | |
| | | | | | | | |
| | | | | | | | |
| | | | | | | | |
| TOTAL | | | | | | | |

## II.16 Participants Checklist

Many people participate in a wedding. Having a list of them in one place assures that you have all roles assigned and that you have contact information when needed. See sections I.3.3, p. 61, and I.4, p. 65 for specifics.

**Checklist 24 – Participants**

| Participant | Name | Phone | Cell Phone |
|---|---|---|---|
| **Wedding Family** | | | |
| Kallah | | | |
| Chosson | | | |
| Kallah's parents | | | |
| Chosson's parents | | | |
| | | | |
| **Vendors** | | | |
| Caterer | | | |
| Baker (wedding cake) | | | |
| Mashgiach | | | |
| Hall sales rep | | | |
| Hall manager | | | |
| Invitation printer | | | |
| Bencher printer | | | |
| Orchestra | | | |
| Photographer | | | |
| Videographer | | | |
| Florist | | | |
| Seamstress | | | |
| Hair stylist | | | |
| Makeup stylist | | | |
| | | | |
| **Helpers** | | | |
| Wedding coordinator | | | |
| Babysitters | | | |
| | | | |
| | | | |
| Ushers | | | |
| | | | |
| | | | |
| Announcer | | | |
| Transportation coordinator | | | |

*The Orthodox Jewish Wedding Planner –*

| Participant | Name | Phone | Cell Phone |
|---|---|---|---|
| **Honorees** | | | |
| Arev kablan (chosson) | | | |
| Arev kablan (kallah) | | | |
| Eidei tenaim (2) | | | |
| | | | |
| Eidei kethuba (2) | | | |
| | | | |
| Eidei yichud (2) | | | |
| | | | |
| Reading the tenaim | | | |
| | | | |
| **Honorees Announced Under the Chuppah (Give copy to announcer)** | | | |
| Mesader kiddushin | | | |
| Eidei kiddushin (2) | | | |
| | | | |
| Reading the kethuba | | | |
| Chuppah blessing 1 | | | |
| Chuppah blessing 2 | | | |
| Chuppah blessing 3 | | | |
| Chuppah blessing 4 | | | |
| Chuppah blessing 5 | | | |
| Chuppah blessing 6 | | | |
| Chuppah blessing 7 | | | |
| | | | |
| Chuppah holders (4) | | | |
| | | | |
| | | | |
| | | | |
| | | | |
| **Chazzans** | | | |
| Mi Adir | | | |
| Min Bon Siach | | | |
| Im Eshkachech | | | |
| | | | |
| **Processional** | | | |
| Groomsmen | | | |
| | | | |
| | | | |
| Siblings (chosson) | | | |
| | | | |
| | | | |

- 120 -

| Participant | Name | Phone | Cell Phone |
|---|---|---|---|
| Grandparents (chosson) | | | |
| Bridesmaids | | | |
| Siblings (kallah) | | | |
| Grandparents (kallah) | | | |
| Flower girl | | | |
| Ring bearer | | | |
| | | | |
| **Reception** | | | |
| Sheva brachos 1 | | | |
| Sheva brachos 2 | | | |
| Sheva brachos 3 | | | |
| Sheva brachos 4 | | | |
| Sheva brachos 5 | | | |
| Sheva brachos 6 | | | |
| Sheva brachos 7 (also leads the meal blessings) | | | |
| | | | |
| Backup | | | |
| Backup | | | |
| Backup | | | |

*The Orthodox Jewish Wedding Planner –*

## II.17 Announcer Responsibilities Checklist

As mentioned in section I.4, p. 65, you may need a lot of help under the chuppah to keep things running smoothly. This list identifies the responsibilities and allows you to assign each one.

**Checklist 25 – Announcer Responsibilities**

| Done | Item | Assigned To… |
|---|---|---|
|  | Prepare items for chuppah |  |
|  |     Kittel and tallis |  |
|  |     Wine and wineglass |  |
|  |     Cards or siddur for the sheva brachos |  |
|  |     Glass to break |  |
|  |     Table for the above items |  |
|  | Verify that those who are to get honors (or their backups) are present |  |
|  | Remind guests to turn off cell phones and refrain from talking during the chuppah ceremony |  |
|  | Take the candles from the parents after they arrive at the chuppah |  |
|  | Make sure that the kallah circles the chosson in the correct direction – counterclockwise |  |
|  | Keep count to be sure that the kallah circles the chosson seven times |  |
|  | Position the microphone so that the guests can hear the proceedings |  |
|  | Announce honorees |  |
|  | Take responsibility for the kethuba after it is given to the kallah |  |
|  | Take care of kittel and other items left after the chuppah ceremony |  |
|  |  |  |
|  |  |  |

# II.18 What to Bring Checklist

There are lots of things to bring on the day of the wedding. Here is a list to help you remember. Simply cross off those things that others are bringing.

**Checklist 26 – What to Bring**

|   | Item |
|---|---|
| **Needed Before the Chuppah** | |
|   | Wedding gown, veil, shoes… |
|   | Kethuba (and extra copies) |
|   | Tenaim (and extra copies) |
|   | Pre-nups |
|   | Marriage license / marriage certificate |
|   | Plate for mothers to break, Nifty Plate Smasher (p. 79) |
|   | Seating lists |
|   | Seating charts (ordered by name and by table) |
|   | Organizational lists (honorees, seating…) |
|   | Preparation basket and quick-fix supplies |
|   | |
| **For the Chuppah** | |
|   | Chuppah |
|   | Tallis |
|   | Overcoat for chosson |
|   | Kittel |
|   | Ashes |
|   | Candles |
|   | Siddur or cards with sheva brachos |
|   | Programs |
|   | Wedding ring |
|   | Wine and cups for chuppah |
|   | Glass to step on |
|   | Chuppah mints |
|   | Silver spoon – See Yichud, p. 28 |
|   | |
| **Needed for After Chuppah** | |
|   | Chairs for chosson and kallah |
|   | Shtick, favors |
|   | Siddurim |
|   | Benchers |
|   | Wine and glasses for sheva brachos |
|   | Checks to pay service providers |
|   | Box for cards and gifts |
|   | |

*The Orthodox Jewish Wedding Planner –*

## II.19 Sheva Brachos Checklists

As mentioned in section I.5.3, p. 75, ideally, many of the sheva brachos will be prepared by others. The first list will help organize the overall sheva brachos schedule. Specific lists for each sheva brachos can be given to those organizing them.

### *Sheva Brachos Schedule*

Use this list to keep the overall schedule of sheva brachos for the entire week.

**Checklist 27 – Sheva Brachos Schedule**

| Day | Time | Organizer | Phone | Location |
|---|---|---|---|---|
| | | | | |
| | | | | |
| | | | | |
| | | | | |
| | | | | |
| | | | | |
| | | | | |
| | | | | |
| | | | | |
| | | | | |
| | | | | |
| | | | | |
| | | | | |
| | | | | |

*Part II – Checklists*

## Sheva Brachos Guest List

This list can be used by each person organizing a single sheva brachos meal. Some specific columns are described below.

- **Minyan** – This indicates that the person can be counted as one of the ten men required for sheva brachos. It is prudent to have more than the required ten in case someone is unable attend unexpectedly.
- **Speaking** – This indicates that the person will say a few words during the meal to the chosson and kallah.
- **Participant** – This is someone who helped with the preparation of the sheva brachos. This is useful when the host is thanking all of those that helped.
- **Bracha** – This is a number from one to seven indicating who will recite which blessing during the benching. Note that the last bracha is said by the one who leads the benching.

**Checklist 28 – Sheva Brachos Guests**

| Guest | Phone | Minyan | Speaking | Participant | Bracha |
|---|---|---|---|---|---|
| Chosson and kallah | | ✓ | | | |
| | | | | | |
| | | | | | |
| | | | | | |
| | | | | | |
| | | | | | |
| | | | | | |
| | | | | | |
| | | | | | |
| | | | | | |
| | | | | | |
| | | | | | |
| | | | | | |
| | | | | | |
| | | | | | |
| | | | | | |
| | | | | | |
| | | | | | |
| | | | | | |
| | | | | | |
| | | | | | |
| | | | | | |
| | | | | | |
| | | | | | |

*The Orthodox Jewish Wedding Planner –*

## Sheva Brachos Guest Suggestions

Those organizing sheva brachos may want suggestions as to whom to invite. For example, these may be friends and relatives who, for whatever reason, could not attend the wedding.

- **Relationship**: How this person is related to the couple, e.g., "friend of the chosson."
- **Sheva brachos**: To which sheva brachos this person was invited.

**Checklist 29 – Sheva Brachos Guest Suggestions**

| Guest | Phone | Relationship | Sheva Brachos |
|---|---|---|---|
| | | | |
| | | | |
| | | | |
| | | | |
| | | | |
| | | | |
| | | | |
| | | | |
| | | | |
| | | | |
| | | | |
| | | | |
| | | | |
| | | | |
| | | | |
| | | | |
| | | | |
| | | | |
| | | | |
| | | | |
| | | | |
| | | | |
| | | | |
| | | | |
| | | | |

# Part III – Blessings

## III.1 Badeken

At the badeken, the chosson places the veil on the kallah. Then the father of the kallah and the father of the chosson (in that order) bless the kallah as follows.

**Blessings 1 – Fathers to the Kallah at the Badeken**

> אֲחֹתֵנוּ, אַתְּ הֲיִי לְאַלְפֵי רְבָבָה,
> וְיִירַשׁ זַרְעֵךְ אֵת שַׁעַר שֹׂנְאָיו.
> יְשִׂימֵךְ אֱלֹהִים כְּשָׂרָה, רִבְקָה,
> רָחֵל וְלֵאָה.

The first phrase is from *Genesis 24:60*. The second phrase is suggestive of *Genesis 48:20*. Some fathers include the priestly blessing at this point as well.

**Blessings 2 – Fathers to the Kallah at the Badeken – The Priestly Blessing**

> יְבָרֶכְךָ יְיָ וְיִשְׁמְרֶךָ.
> יָאֵר יְיָ פָּנָיו אֵלֶיךָ וִיחֻנֶּךָּ.
> יִשָּׂא יְיָ פָּנָיו אֵלֶיךָ, וְיָשֵׂם לְךָ שָׁלוֹם.

*The Orthodox Jewish Wedding Planner –*

## III.2 Chuppah

When the chosson reaches the chuppah, the following is sung.

**Blessings 3 – When the Chosson Arrives at the Chuppah**

> בָּרוּךְ הַבָּא.
> מִי אַדִּיר עַל הַכֹּל, מִי בָּרוּךְ עַל הַכֹּל,
> מִי גָּדוֹל עַל הַכֹּל, מִי דָּגוּל עַל הַכֹּל,
> הוּא יְבָרֵךְ אֶת הֶחָתָן וְאֶת הַכַּלָּה.

**Blessings 4 – When the Chosson Arrives at the Chuppah (German Custom)**

> בָּרוּךְ הַבָּא בְּשֵׁם יְיָ, בֵּרַכְנוּכֶם מִבֵּית יְיָ.
> אֵל יְיָ וַיָּאֶר לָנוּ, אִסְרוּ חַג בַּעֲבֹתִים, עַד קַרְנוֹת הַמִּזְבֵּחַ.
> אֵלִי אַתָּה וְאוֹדֶךָּ, אֱלֹהַי אֲרוֹמְמֶךָּ.
> הוֹדוּ לַייָ כִּי טוֹב, כִּי לְעוֹלָם חַסְדּוֹ.

When the kallah reaches the chuppah and proceeds to circle the chosson seven times, the following is sung.

**Blessings 5 – When the Kallah Arrives at the Chuppah**

> בְּרוּכָה הַבָּאָה.
> מִי בֶן שִׂיחַ שׁוֹשָׁן חוֹחִים,
> אַהֲבַת כַּלָּה מְשׂוֹשׂ דּוֹדִים,
> הוּא יְבָרֵךְ אֶת הֶחָתָן וְאֶת הַכַּלָּה.

The mesader kiddushin will say the following at the appropriate point.

**Blessings 6 – Erusin**

> בָּרוּךְ אַתָּה יְיָ אֱלֹהֵינוּ מֶלֶךְ הָעוֹלָם, בּוֹרֵא פְּרִי הַגָּפֶן.
>
> בָּרוּךְ אַתָּה יְיָ אֱלֹהֵינוּ מֶלֶךְ הָעוֹלָם, אֲשֶׁר קִדְּשָׁנוּ בְּמִצְוֹתָיו,
> וְצִוָּנוּ עַל הָעֲרָיוֹת, וְאָסַר לָנוּ אֶת הָאֲרוּסוֹת,
> וְהִתִּיר לָנוּ אֶת הַנְּשׂוּאוֹת לָנוּ עַל יְדֵי חֻפָּה וְקִדּוּשִׁין.
> בָּרוּךְ אַתָּה יְיָ, מְקַדֵּשׁ עַמּוֹ יִשְׂרָאֵל עַל יְדֵי חֻפָּה וְקִדּוּשִׁין.

The chosson says the following and then immediately places the ring on the right index finger of the kallah.

## Part III – Blessings

**Blessings 7 – The Chosson Gives the Kallah the Ring**

> הֲרֵי אַתְּ מְקוּדֶּשֶׁת לִי, בְּטַבַּעַת זוֹ, כְּדַת מֹשֶׁה וְיִשְׂרָאֵל.

Under the chuppah the sheva brachos are said. Since sheva brachos are said both under the chuppah and at each sheva brachos meal, they are listed on their own page. See Blessings 10, page 132.

After the last of the sheva brachos, before the chosson steps on the glass, the following excerpt from *Psalms 137:5-6* is often sung.

**Blessings 8 – Before Breaking the Glass**

> אִם אֶשְׁכָּחֵךְ יְרוּשָׁלָיִם, תִּשְׁכַּח יְמִינִי.
> תִּדְבַּק לְשׁוֹנִי לְחִכִּי, אִם לֹא אֶזְכְּרֵכִי.
> אִם לֹא אַעֲלֶה אֶת יְרוּשָׁלַיִם עַל רֹאשׁ שִׂמְחָתִי.

The German custom is to sing Psalm 128.

**Blessings 9 – German Custom before Breaking Glass**

> שִׁיר הַמַּעֲלוֹת; אַשְׁרֵי כָּל יְרֵא יְיָ, הַהֹלֵךְ בִּדְרָכָיו.
> יְגִיעַ כַּפֶּיךָ כִּי תֹאכֵל, אַשְׁרֶיךָ וְטוֹב לָךְ. אֶשְׁתְּךָ
> כְּגֶפֶן פֹּרִיָּה בְּיַרְכְּתֵי בֵיתֶךָ; בָּנֶיךָ כִּשְׁתִלֵי זֵיתִים
> סָבִיב לְשֻׁלְחָנֶךָ. הִנֵּה כִי כֵן יְבֹרַךְ גָּבֶר יְרֵא יְיָ.
> יְבָרֶכְךָ יְיָ מִצִּיּוֹן, וּרְאֵה בְּטוּב יְרוּשָׁלָיִם כֹּל יְמֵי
> חַיֶּיךָ. וּרְאֵה בָנִים לְבָנֶיךָ, שָׁלוֹם עַל יִשְׂרָאֵל.

## III.3 Sheva Brachos

Note that the order of the blessings under the chuppah is different than the order said at the sheva brachos meals.

**Blessings 10 – Sheva Brachos**

| Chuppah | Brachos | Sheva Brachos Meal |
|---|---|---|
| 1 | בָּרוּךְ אַתָּה יְיָ אֱלֹהֵינוּ מֶלֶךְ הָעוֹלָם, בּוֹרֵא פְּרִי הַגָּפֶן. | Said Last |
| 2 | בָּרוּךְ אַתָּה יְיָ אֱלֹהֵינוּ מֶלֶךְ הָעוֹלָם, שֶׁהַכֹּל בָּרָא לִכְבוֹדוֹ. | 1 |
| 3 | בָּרוּךְ אַתָּה יְיָ אֱלֹהֵינוּ מֶלֶךְ הָעוֹלָם, יוֹצֵר הָאָדָם. | 2 |
| 4 | בָּרוּךְ אַתָּה יְיָ אֱלֹהֵינוּ מֶלֶךְ הָעוֹלָם, אֲשֶׁר יָצַר אֶת הָאָדָם בְּצַלְמוֹ, בְּצֶלֶם דְּמוּת תַּבְנִיתוֹ, וְהִתְקִין לוֹ מִמֶּנּוּ בִּנְיַן עֲדֵי עַד. בָּרוּךְ אַתָּה יְיָ יוֹצֵר הָאָדָם. | 3 |
| 5 | שׂוֹשׂ תָּשִׂישׂ וְתָגֵל הָעֲקָרָה, בְּקִבּוּץ בָּנֶיהָ לְתוֹכָהּ בְּשִׂמְחָה. בָּרוּךְ אַתָּה יְיָ, מְשַׂמֵּחַ צִיּוֹן בְּבָנֶיהָ. | 4 |
| 6 | שַׂמֵּחַ תְּשַׂמַּח רֵעִים הָאֲהוּבִים, כְּשַׂמֵּחֲךָ יְצִירְךָ בְּגַן עֵדֶן מִקֶּדֶם. בָּרוּךְ אַתָּה יְיָ, מְשַׂמֵּחַ חָתָן וְכַלָּה. | 5 |
| 7 | בָּרוּךְ אַתָּה יְיָ אֱלֹהֵינוּ מֶלֶךְ הָעוֹלָם, אֲשֶׁר בָּרָא שָׂשׂוֹן וְשִׂמְחָה, חָתָן וְכַלָּה, גִּילָה רִנָּה, דִּיצָה וְחֶדְוָה, אַהֲבָה וְאַחֲוָה, וְשָׁלוֹם וְרֵעוּת. מְהֵרָה יְיָ אֱלֹהֵינוּ יִשָּׁמַע בְּעָרֵי יְהוּדָה וּבְחֻצוֹת יְרוּשָׁלָיִם, קוֹל שָׂשׂוֹן וְקוֹל שִׂמְחָה, קוֹל חָתָן וְקוֹל כַּלָּה, קוֹל מִצְהֲלוֹת חֲתָנִים מֵחֻפָּתָם, וּנְעָרִים מִמִּשְׁתֵּה נְגִינָתָם. בָּרוּךְ אַתָּה יְיָ, מְשַׂמֵּחַ חָתָן עִם הַכַּלָּה. | 6 |
| Said First | בָּרוּךְ אַתָּה יְיָ אֱלֹהֵינוּ מֶלֶךְ הָעוֹלָם, בּוֹרֵא פְּרִי הַגָּפֶן. | 7 |

# III.4 Benching for the Sheva Brachos Meal

Prepare three cups. Fill two with wine (some fill the second cup after benching). Then sing שיר המעלות, which can be found in any standard bencher.

The following is a special introduction to benching for sheva brachos. Most benchers have this text but it is often small or hard to find. The leader holds the first cup during the benching, until בונה ברחמיו ירושלים, אמן. Some Chassidim do not say this introduction on Shabbos, but rather use the regular introduction found in the benchers.

**Blessings 11 – Introduction to Sheva Brachos Benching**

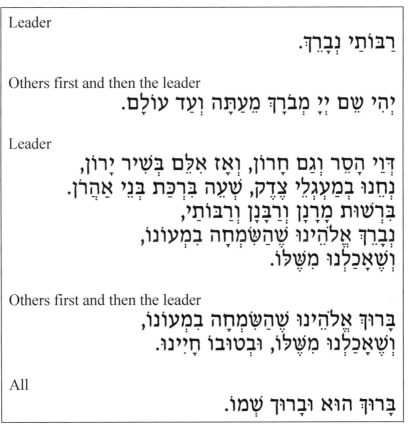

After this introduction, all attending recite benching. After benching, the second cup is passed to six honorees, each of whom holds the cup in their right hand and says one of the first six sheva brachos in order. See Blessings 10, page 132. Then, the one who led the benching recites the last bracha.

After the last blessing:
1. Some wine from cups 1 and 2 is poured into empty cup 3 until it is mostly full.
2. Some of the wine from cup 3 is poured back into cups 1 and 2.
3. The one who led the benching drinks from cup 1.
4. The chosson and kallah each drink from one of the two remaining cups.

*The Orthodox Jewish Wedding Planner –*

The sheva brachos are recited after the meal only if at least one Jewish man has participated who did not attend the wedding meal. According to Sephardic custom, these brachos are only said if at least two such men are in attendance and the meal is in the house of the chosson. Otherwise, only the last two blessings as indicated in Blessings 10 are said.

# Part IV – Reference

*Part IV –Reference*

# IV.1 Glossary

Many Hebrew and Yiddish terms are used throughout this guide. This glossary should help if you are not familiar with some of them. Pronunciation is typically Ashkenazic as opposed to Sephardic. Some Sephardic pronunciations are given if used in the text.

- Aliyah — Honor of being called to the Torah during shul services.
- Arev kablan — A guarantor.
- Ashkenazim — Jews of cultural descent from Eastern Europe (other than Chassidim) (adj. Ashkenazic).
- Av — Fifth of the Jewish calendar months (from Nissan).
- Badeken — Veiling of the kallah by the chosson.
- Bencher — Small prayer book containing the blessings for meals.
- Benching — Blessings after the meal.
- Birchas Cohanim — Blessings that Cohanim bestow on the congregation during holiday services (every day in Israel).
- Bracha — Blessing.
- Chabad — A widespread Chassidic movement centered in Crown Heights, New York.
- Challah — Ceremonial braided loaf of bread (Not to be confused with kallah – see below).
- Chassidim — Jews of cultural descent from one of various groups of Eastern Europe emanating from the Baal Shem Tov of the 1700's (adj. Chassidic).
- Chazzan — Cantor.
- Chosson (chatan) — Bridegroom.
- Chosson mohl — Meal served on the eve of the wedding (literally: chosson's time). See section I.5.3, p. 75.
- Chosson's tisch — Place where chosson greets guests (literally: chosson's table).
- Chuppah — Wedding canopy.
- Cohen — A descendent of Aaron, the brother of Moses, charged with specific ritual duties (pl. Cohanim).
- Daven — Pray.
- Eid — Witness (eidei: witnesses of…).
- Erusin — The first stage of marriage followed by nesuin.
- Gemach — Abbreviation for gemilath chassadim, which means acts of kindness. A service run by an individual or organization that loans items to the public.
- Haftorah — A portion read from the Prophets during Shabbos morning services.
- Halacha — Jewish law (adj. halachic).
- Hallel — A portion of the davening recited on holidays.
- Hashem — G-d (literally: The Name).

- Henna — Specifically, a plant producing a dying agent. Generally, a Sephardic event prior to the wedding. See section I.5.3, p. 75.
- Kabbalas panim — Greeting guests. Separate receptions prior to the wedding ceremony for the chosson and kallah.
- Kallah — Bride.
- Kasher — To bring cooking facilities into compliance with Jewish dietary laws for the preparation of food.
- Kethuba — Marriage contract.
- Kiddush — Reception following shul services on Shabbos morning.
- Kiddushin — First stage of marriage (same as erusin).
- Kippah — Religious cap worn by Jewish men (pl. kippoth).
- Kinyan — Formal acquisition (pl. kinyanim).
- Kittel — Simple white robe worn by the chosson under the chuppah.
- Kosher — Complying with Jewish dietary laws.
- L'chayim — An immediate reception for the chosson and kallah on the night of the engagement (literally: To Life!).
- Lubavitch — See Chabad.
- Maariv — Evening prayer service.
- Mashgiach — Agent of the kosher supervision authority.
- Mechitza — A room divider.
- Mesader kiddushin — The officiating rabbi at the wedding ceremony.
- Mezinke tanz — A dance honoring parents who have married off their last child. See section I.1.4, p. 23.
- Mikveh — Ritual bath.
- Mincha — Afternoon prayer service.
- Minyan — Quorum of ten Jewish men required for communal prayers (pl. minyanim).
- Mitzvah — Commandment.
- Nesuin — The second stage of marriage preceded by erusin.
- Nissan — First of the Jewish calendar months.
- Rabbenu Gershom — Leader of the Ashkenazic Jewish community during the 10th century.
- Segula — An action or item believed to possess auspicious metaphysical significance.
- Sephardim — Jews of cultural descent from Southern Europe, the Middle East or Northern Africa (adj. Sephardic).
- Shabbos (Shabbat) — Sabbath.
- Shabbas Kallah — An informal reception held for the kallah on the Shabbos preceding the wedding. See Shabbos Kallah, p. 76.
- Shadchun — Matchmaker.
- Shalosh seudos — The third Shabbos meal.
- Shatnes — The forbidden mixture of linen and wool in clothing.
- Sheitel — Wig.

*Part IV – Reference*

- Sheva brachos — The seven marriage blessings recited under the chuppah and at meals following the wedding. Also, a meal at which these blessings are recited.
- Sheva p'ruta — Worth a minimal monetary value (literally: equivalent to a p'ruta).
- Shevuoth — Feast of Weeks (seven weeks after Passover).
- Shtar chalitza — Document enjoining brothers of the chosson to perform the rite of release in the event the chosson passes without children. See Shtar Chalitza, p. 30.
- Shtick — A gimmick for entertainment.
- Shul — Synagogue.
- Siddur — Prayer book (pl. siddurim).
- Simcha — Joyous occasion.
- Streimel — Fur hat worn by some Chassidic sects.
- Tachnun — A specific section of prayers, containing supplications for forgiveness, recited during regular services.
- Tallis — Prayer shawl.
- Talmud — Compilation of the oral tradition (adj. talmudic).
- Tamuz — Fourth of the Jewish calendar months (from Nissan).
- Tanz — Dance.
- Tenaim — Document containing conditions of engagement.
- Torah — The Written Law, the Five Books of Moses.
- Ufruf — The aliyah given to the chosson on the Shabbos before the wedding (Literally: calling up).
- Viduy — Prayers of confession.
- Vort — An engagement reception for the couple; typically held one or more weeks after the engagement (literally: word).
- Yeshiva — Seminary where men study Jewish law.
- Yichud — The first seclusion of the chosson and kallah after the chuppah.
- Yom Kippur — The Day of Atonement.
- Z'tl — Abbreviation for zecher tzadik l'vracha – May the mention of the righteous one be for a blessing.

*The Orthodox Jewish Wedding Planner –*

## IV.2  Artwork Credits

This section identifies those who contributed photographs and drawings to this guide. Artwork not identified here was prepared by the author.

| | |
|---|---|
| Cover Drawings | Mrs. Natanya Nudelman |
| Photo 5, p. 37 | Mr. Tzvi Wygoda |
| Photo 12, p. 74 | Mr. Avraham Bank |
| Photo 14, p. 79 (Left) | Mr. Tzvi Wygoda |

## IV.3  Citations

**Sefarim (Hebrew Books)**

[א] ספר חופה וקדושין, הר' יצחק יוסף, תשס"ה
[ב] ספר והייתם קדושים, הר' לבי יצחק הלבי הורוויץ, תשס"ד
[ג] הלכות והליכות אירוסין ונשואין השלם, הר' שמואל אליעזר שטרן, תשנ"ט

**Web Sites**

[1] www.usps.com
United States Postal Service

[2] www.upu.int/members/en/ members.html
Universal Postal Union – Member Countries

[3] www.orientaltrading.com
Oriental Trading gift items

[4] Moreshetashkenaz.com
The Institute for Ashkenazi Heritage

[5] www.hennapage.com
Information about Henna

[6] www.chabad.org/480435
Melody of the Four Stanzas

[7] jewishweddings.home.mindspring.com
Official Web site for this guide – melody samples, links and more

[8] jewishweddings.home.mindspring.com/etiquette.html
Etiquette article

*Part IV – Reference*

# Checklist Quick Reference

Checklist 1 – The Main Point ................................................................................ 12
Checklist 2 – Timing ............................................................................................. 88
Checklist 3 – Choosing a Date .............................................................................. 90
Checklist 4 – Wedding Scope ............................................................................... 91
Checklist 5 – Wedding Cost Details ..................................................................... 91
Checklist 6 – Customs ........................................................................................... 92
Checklist 7 – Selecting a Hall ............................................................................... 94
Checklist 8 – Selecting a Caterer .......................................................................... 97
Checklist 9 – Selecting a Florist ........................................................................... 99
Checklist 10 – Selecting an Orchestra ................................................................ 101
Checklist 11 – Selecting a Photographer ............................................................ 103
Checklist 12 – Selecting a Videographer ........................................................... 105
Checklist 13 – Poses ........................................................................................... 106
Checklist 14 – Guest List Sample ....................................................................... 108
Checklist 15 – Seating List Sample .................................................................... 110
Checklist 16 – Selecting an Invitation Printer .................................................... 111
Checklist 17 – Invitation Information ................................................................. 112
Checklist 18 – Invitation Content ....................................................................... 113
Checklist 19 – Wardrobe .................................................................................... 114
Checklist 20 – Documentation ............................................................................ 115
Checklist 21 – Accommodations ........................................................................ 116
Checklist 22 – Chartering a Bus ......................................................................... 117
Checklist 23 – Bus Passengers ........................................................................... 118
Checklist 24 – Participants ................................................................................. 119
Checklist 25 – Announcer Responsibilities ........................................................ 122
Checklist 26 – What to Bring ............................................................................. 123
Checklist 27 – Sheva Brachos Schedule ............................................................. 124
Checklist 28 – Sheva Brachos Guests ................................................................. 125
Checklist 29 – Sheva Brachos Guest Suggestions .............................................. 126

Made in the USA
Middletown, DE
17 February 2020